Cambridge Elements

Behavioural and Experimental Economics
edited by
Nicolas Jacquemet
University Paris-1 Panthéon Sorbonne and the Paris School of Economics
Olivier L'Haridon
Université de Rennes 1

T0286908

IMPERFECT PERCEPTION AND STOCHASTIC CHOICE IN EXPERIMENTS

Pablo Brañas-Garza
Loyola University Andalusia

John Smith
Rutgers University-Camden

CAMBRIDGE
UNIVERSITY PRESS

Shaftesbury Road, Cambridge CB2 8EA, United Kingdom

One Liberty Plaza, 20th Floor, New York, NY 10006, USA

477 Williamstown Road, Port Melbourne, VIC 3207, Australia

314–321, 3rd Floor, Plot 3, Splendor Forum, Jasola District Centre, New Delhi – 110025, India

103 Penang Road, #05–06/07, Visioncrest Commercial, Singapore 238467

Cambridge University Press is part of Cambridge University Press & Assessment, a department of the University of Cambridge.

We share the University's mission to contribute to society through the pursuit of education, learning and research at the highest international levels of excellence.

www.cambridge.org
Information on this title: www.cambridge.org/9781009454414

DOI: 10.1017/9781009049207

First published 2023

A catalogue record for this publication is available from the British Library

ISBN 978-1-009-45441-4 Hardback
ISBN 978-1-009-04869-9 Paperback
ISSN 2634-1824 (online)
ISSN 2634-1816 (print)

Imperfect Perception and Stochastic Choice in Experiments

Behavioural and Experimental Economics

DOI: 10.1017/9781009049207
First published online: December 2023

Pablo Brañas-Garza
Loyola University Andalusia

John Smith
Rutgers University-Camden

Author for correspondence: John Smith, smithj@camden.rutgers.edu

Abstract: The branch of psychology that studies how physical objects are perceived by subjects is known as psychophysics. A feature of the experimental design is that the experimenter presents objectively measurable objects that are imperfectly perceived by subjects. The responses are stochastic in that a subject might respond differently in otherwise identical situations. These stochastic choices can be compared to the objectively measurable properties. This Element offers a brief introduction to the topic, explains how psychophysics insights are already present in economics, and describes experimental techniques with the goal that they are useful in the design of economics experiments. Noise is a ubiquitous feature of experimental economics and there is a large strand of economics literature that carefully considers the noise. However, the authors view the psychophysics experimental techniques as uniquely suited to helping experimental economists uncover what is hiding in the noise.

Keywords: experimental economics, psychophysics, random choice, psychology and economics, psychometric function

ISBNs: 9781009454414 (HB), 9781009048699 (PB), 9781009049207 (OC)
ISSNs: 2634-1824 (online), 2634-1816 (print)

Contents

1 The Apparently Random Coffee Purchases of a Colleague

Suppose that you make repeated observations about whether a colleague buys coffee at a café on the way to work. The colleague knows both the quality and the price of the coffee. Therefore, there is neither learning nor external risk. You observe that the colleague buys a coffee (which we denote as A) on some days. However, on other days, the colleague walks past the café and does not buy a coffee (which we denote as B).

The classical view is that economic choice is deterministic: if the utility of $A(U_A)$ is greater than the utility of $B(U_B)$, then A is selected over B with certainty. Consequently, when A is chosen (over B), then we infer that U_A is larger than U_B. Figure 1 characterizes both classical economic choice and economic inference.

To model the setting, an analyst could estimate the utility of $A(\hat{U}_A)$ and the utility of $B(\hat{U}_B)$ from the information available. However, because these estimates of the utilities are imperfect, the analyst will include error terms, which can be interpreted as accounting for information not available to the experimenter but available to the decision-maker (McFadden, 1974, 2001). In this view, the decision-maker acts as described in Figure 1. However, the analyst models the utilities as $\hat{U}_A + \varepsilon_A$ and $\hat{U}_B + \varepsilon_B$ and assumes that the decision-maker selects the option with the largest realized value. Even if utility is random from the perspective of the analyst and not the decision-maker, this specification can be referred to as a *random utility model*.

In order to motivate the randomness, *private information explanations* suggest that the decision-maker has private information that is not observable to the experimenter, and this accounts for the apparently random choice.[1] This is part of the more general effort to handle situations where the analyst does not have access to all of the relevant information.[2]

Suppose that B was selected today. An explanation consistent with private information would be that the colleague had coffee earlier in the morning and this was not observable to you.[3]

Despite the success of these random utility models, evidence has been accumulating that the behavior described in Figure 1 is not descriptively accurate: many of the choices in economic settings are apparently random from the

---

[1] For example, see Lu (2016).

[2] Other examples of this vast literature include McFadden (1974), Hausman and Wise (1978), Rodríguez, Urzúa, and Reyes (2016), Wooldridge (2019), and Brañas-Garza, Ductor, and Kovářík (2022). See Train (2009) for a text-length treatment.

[3] The (unobserved) caffeinated state of the colleague is only one such explanation. Consider *wealth effects* where exogenous changes in wealth cause changes in consumption. These wealth effects might also be unobservable to the analyst. For example, it is possible that the colleague's financial portfolio lost value or a neighbor's house sold for an unexpectedly small amount. See Case, Quigley, and Shiller (2005) for more on wealth effects.

(a) Economic choice	(b) Economic inference
$U_A > U_B \rightarrow A$ is chosen (over B)	When A is chosen (over B) $\rightarrow U_A > U_B$
$U_A = U_B \rightarrow$ random choice	When random choice $\rightarrow U_A = U_B$
$U_A < U_B \rightarrow B$ is chosen (over A)	When B is chosen (over A) $\rightarrow U_B > U_A$

Figure 1 A characterization of classical economic choice and economic inference. If U_A is the utility from option A and U_B is the utility from option B, Panel (a) describes the predictions of choice between A and B. Panel (b) describes the inferences of U_A and U_B based on the choice between A and B.

perspective of the decision-maker. For example, subjects[4] often select options from choice sets, which, by their own descriptions, are less desirable than available options (Reutskaja et al., 2011). Additionally, when a subject is given an identical choice set, different choices are observed (Hey, 1995, 2001; Agranov and Ortoleva, 2017). In fact, such noise is ubiquitous in experimental economics, and there is a literature showing the insights that can be gleaned from careful consideration of noise.[5]

Several explanations have emerged that could help explain the *apparent* violations of behavior in Figure 1.

- *Consideration set explanations* (Eliaz and Spiegler, 2011; Masatlioglu, Nakajima, and Ozbay, 2012; Manzini and Mariotti, 2014) contend that subjects do not necessarily consider every element in the choice set but have an unobserved consideration set from which a choice is made. From the perspective of the decision-maker, the best item is selected from the set under consideration. These theoretical efforts were motivated by the marketing literature that examines the implications of consideration sets.[6] In our setting, this could imply that the colleague was possibly distracted – for example, by their phone – and did not consider buying coffee today.
- *Preference for randomization explanations* (Agranov and Ortoleva, 2017; Cerreia-Vioglio et al., 2019) suggests that subjects have a preference for randomization in a way to attain balanced or mixed choices. In fact, many subjects make different choices to the same questions, which are asked

---

[4] In the psychology literature, the term *participant* is currently preferred over *subject* (American Psychological Association, 2010). However, because it is currently more standard in the economics literature, we use the term *subject*.

[5] See Loomes, Starmer, and Sugden (1989), Hey and Orme (1994), Loomes (2005), and Butler and Loomes (2007) for early contributions. See Apesteguia, Ballester, and Lu (2017), Liang (2019), Bayrak and Hey (2020), Alós-Ferrer and Garagnani (2021), Apesteguia and Ballester (2021), and Amador-Hidalgo et al. (2021) for more recent contributions.

[6] See Shocker et al. (1991) and Roberts and Lattin (1991).

consecutively, and subjects are informed of this prior to the questions. In our setting, this could imply the possibility that the colleague was less inclined to purchase coffee today because of recent coffee purchases on previous days.[7]

While these (and still other) explanations can help us understand apparent violations of Figure 1, a somewhat more general explanation is that subjects have stable, well-defined preferences, but they are perceived imperfectly (Luce, 1959).

For example, you ask the colleague about their choice of B and they confess that it was not immediately clear whether they wanted coffee or not. It was only after deliberation that the colleague decided to select B. An explanation consistent with this is that the colleague had objective magnitudes representing the valuations of A and B in their head, but these were only imperfectly observed.

In this case, the colleague's decision could be modeled by underlying preferences, but the choice was affected by noisy perception of these preferences. For example, we could model the situation as the colleague having utilities U_A and U_B. However, these utilities are imperfectly perceived. Specifically, there is an additive noise associated with $A(\varepsilon_A)$ and $B(\varepsilon_B)$. As a result, the colleague only observes $V_A = U_A + \varepsilon_A$ and $V_B = U_B + \varepsilon_B$ and selects the option with the largest realized value. Because ε_A and ε_B are random variables, the choice of A and B will be stochastic: sometimes A will be selected and sometimes B will be selected. Figure 2 characterizes both choice and inference in random utility models with this interpretation of the noise.[8]

(a) Random utility choice	(b) Random utility inference
$U_A + \varepsilon_A > U_B + \varepsilon_B \rightarrow A$ is chosen (over B)	When A is chosen (over B) $\rightarrow U_A + \varepsilon_A > U_B + \varepsilon_B$
$U_A + \varepsilon_A = U_B + \varepsilon_B \rightarrow$ indifferent	Indifferent $\rightarrow U_A + \varepsilon_A = U_B + \varepsilon_B$
$U_A + \varepsilon_A < U_B + \varepsilon_B \rightarrow B$ is chosen (over A)	When B is chosen (over A) $\rightarrow U_A + \varepsilon_A < U_B + \varepsilon_B$

Figure 2 A characterization of choice and inference in a random utility model. The utility of $A(B)$ is $U_A(U_B)$, but this is imperfectly perceived by the decision-maker. This imperfect precision is modeled by additive noises ε_A and ε_B. Panel (a) describes the predictions of random choice and Panel (b) describes the inference of the random utility.

---

[7] More broadly, there is a literature that employs models where consumption in previous periods affects preferences in the current period. Examples of this *habit formation* literature are Boldrin, Christiano, and Fisher (2001), Rozen (2010), Rustichini and Siconolfi (2014), and Tserenjigmid (2020), including habit effects in the demand for coffee (Okunade, 1992).

[8] Since evidence of the preference for randomization occurs in settings where the subjects are close to indifference (Agranov and Ortoleva, 2017), it can be difficult to distinguish between a preference for randomization and a random utility model where errors vary across adjacent trials.

However, a hindrance in studying the role of imperfect perception on random choice in economics is that the true preferences (U_A and U_B) are either not observed or are only imperfectly measured (through self-reported rankings, elicited willingness to pay, expected utility estimates, etc.).

By contrast, the psychology literature has long employed a technique whereby researchers know the exact objective measure of a *stimulus*[9] that is imperfectly perceived by subjects (Weber, 1834; Fechner, 1860). An example would be presenting subjects with two weights and asking which is heavier. Because the weights are imperfectly perceived, the response will be stochastic. Suppose that the weights are 2.0 kg and 1.9 kg. On some trials, the subject will declare the 2.0 kg weight to be heavier and on other trials the subject will declare the 1.9 kg weight to be heavier. Because the experimenter knows the objective values, an unambiguous determination can be made about the optimality of the judgment.

It is also the case that the probability of a correct response will tend to be increasing in the difference between the weights. Suppose, instead, that the weights were 2.0 kg and 1.5 kg. The responses will still be stochastic, but the probability that the 2.0 kg weight is declared heavier than the 1.5 kg weight will be larger than the probability that the 2.0 kg weight is declared heavier than the 1.9 kg weight. In general, there will be a positive relationship between correctly identifying the more intense stimulus and the differences between the stimuli (Kingdom and Prins, 2016, ch. 2).

More broadly, there is a large effort to better understand the relationship between objectively measurable physical stimuli and how they are experienced and perceived. Because this literature combines the *psychological* and the *physical*, it is referred to as *psychophysics*.[10] Although this psychophysics literature is largely not incentivized,[11] it can be modified to conform to the conventions of modern experimental economics by making payments contingent on the object- ive – but imperfectly perceived – features of choice objects.[12] This is a technique to generate apparently random behavior in experimental subjects that would permit a direct comparison of the probability of an optimal choice and the objective features of the choice problem.

In other words, when the researcher knows the objectively optimal choice, the noise provides clues that are not available when the optimal choice is not

---

[9] This word might seem unusual to the economist reader. By *stimulus* we mean the event or the object presented to subjects in order to observe their response. The plural of stimulus is stimuli.

[10] See Falmagne (2002) for an excellent treatment of psychophysics theory.

[11] In the following, we discuss the growing literature that employs this technique of providing material incentives in choice settings with imperfectly perceived stimuli.

[12] Experimental economists have been inducing values in economic experiments for many years (Smith, 1976).

known. Hence, the technique can provide clues about what is hiding in the noise. Experiment 1 provides an example of such a design.

EXPERIMENT 1: Consider a design where subjects are instructed to choose between two lines and payoffs are proportional to the length of the selected line. Subjects will try to select the longer of the lines. Since the lengths of the lines are known to the experimenter, the probability of an optimal choice can be informed by the objective aspects of the setting, including the lengths of the two lines.

While the choice in Experiment 1 is likely to be noisy, important clues can be gleaned about the choice because the objective measures of the setting are known. Here, we highlight an attractive feature of that experimental design.

In both the coffee and the line length settings, a subject is making a choice between two elements with objective and nonrandom values (U_A and U_B). Figure 3 depicts a characterization of the difference between the objective line length experiment of Experiment 1 and the observations of the coffee purchases of your colleague. In both settings, the subject observes the subjective values (V_A and V_B), which are noisy signals of the objective and nonrandom values. After observing the subjective values, the subject makes a decision. The experimenter can observe the choice. However, in the line experiment, the analyst has a measure of the objective values accruing to the subject because the values are induced. We concede that in the line length experiment, while the experimenter knows the precise material payments associated with the choices, the utility of the payments are not observed. However, with a monotonicity argument, the experimenter is certain about the optimality of the choice and the differences in their values.

Let us return to the café where we do not have an objective measure of valuations and, therefore, cannot make objective statements about U_A and U_B. Suppose that you supplement your observations of choice with nonchoice data. For example, you can observe the response time, the location of the colleague's gaze, etc. These observations can provide important clues about the colleague's decision process.

Today, the colleague paused in front of the café but, after 20 seconds, resumed the walk toward the office. This behavior could suggest that the relative attractiveness of A and B was imperfectly known because the optimal choice was apparently not even obvious to the colleague. It was only after 20 seconds of deliberation that the colleague arrived at a decision. The colleague was not only deciding *what* to decide (A or B) but also *when* the decision was to be made.

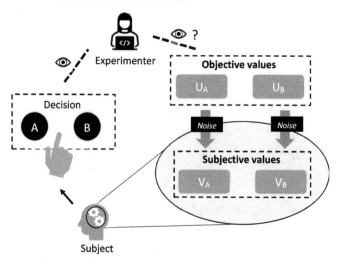

Figure 3 A characterization of a choice experiment, where a subject chooses between *A* and *B*. There are objective and nonrandom values U_A and U_B that are imperfectly perceived as subjective values V_A and V_B. The subject selects the option with the larger subjective value. The analyst can observe the decision. The analyst can observe the objective values in the line example. However, the analyst cannot observe the objective values in the coffee example.

When the attractiveness of the objects in the choice problem is imperfectly known to the experimenter, nonchoice data can shed light on both the attractiveness of the objects in the choice problem and the decision process of the subject. For example, researchers can infer from longer response times that the choice options are closer to indifference (Alós-Ferrer, Fehr, and Netzer, 2021).

However, when the attractiveness of the objects in the choice problem is known by the experimenter, nonchoice data can greatly assist the researcher in understanding the decision process. Specifically, when the objective features of the decision are known to the experimenter (as in Experiment 2), the choice and nonchoice data can provide valuable tests on evidence accumulation models and decision processes, where *what* to choose is made in tandem with *when* to choose it.[13] We can also make statements about the relationship between response times and the optimality of choices.

Again, knowing the objectively optimal choice allows the experimenter to use the noisy features of the deliberation process to inform the nature of the choice.

---

[13] For example, Ratcliff and Rouder (1998), Fudenberg, Strack, and Strzalecki (2018) and Fudenberg et al. (2020).

EXPERIMENT 2: Consider again a design where subjects are instructed to choose between two lines and payoffs are proportional to the length of the selected line. Because the objective features of the setting (including the line lengths) are known to the experimenter, the noisy response times are not needed in order to infer how close the choice is to indifference. Rather, response times and other nonchoice data can be uniquely devoted to inferring the trial-specific and idiosyncratic deliberation process.

The goal of our contribution is to highlight relevant psychophysics insights that are possibly helpful to economists. We are not the ones who made the first such effort, as we note the excellent overviews of Weber (2004), Caplin (2012), and Woodford (2020). However, our contribution is more focused on describing the experimental techniques to the extent that they could be employed by experimental economists.

The goal of this contribution is to give the experimental economist enough background and motivation to design economics experiments with imperfectly perceived stimuli. In other words, these previous efforts are focused on encouraging the use of psychophysics to improve *models* in economics, and we are focused on encouraging the use of psychophysics to improve *experiments* in economics.

We organize the Element as follows. In Section 2, we offer a brief introduction to the classic psychophysics literature, with particular attention to concepts that might prove useful to experimental economists. In Section 3, we describe the extent to which some psychophysics insights already appear in the theoretical and empirical economics literature. In Section 4, we discuss the models that are difficult to test without the use of psychophysics experimental techniques. In Section 5, we describe incentivized experiments where imperfectly perceived stimuli are presented to subjects. We conclude by suggesting some possible directions for using psychophysics techniques in experimental economics research and candid advice on reading the brain sciences literature.

Earlier, we noted examples in the literature that have made advances in apparently stochastic choice by carefully considering the nature of the noise. The techniques that we describe in this contribution permit a different means of carefully considering the noise. When a measure of the objective values associated with each choice is known by the experimenter, this presents a uniquely powerful experimental tool to better understand what is hiding in the noise.

Brain scientists have been employing distinct designs of *perceptual choice* experiments[14] and *economic choice* experiments.[15] On page 1, Summerfield and Tsetsos (2012) write, "It might be worth considering, for example, that all perceptual decisions are ultimately motivated by reward (or the avoidance of loss) whereas all economic decisions require perceptual appraisal of the alternatives on offer."

Despite this quote, Summerfield and Tsetsos (2012) are less focused on encouraging the merging of the experimental designs and more focused on encouraging the use of techniques of analysis commonly used in one set of designs but not in the other set. Our contribution attempts to make the case to an experimental economics audience that the perceptual decision-making and economic decision-making experimental designs could be merged to the substantial benefit of economics.

2 A Brief Introduction to the Psychophysics Literature

Weber's Law

Research has found that objectively measurable stimuli are imperfectly perceived and an increase in the intensity of the stimuli will not necessarily produce a linear increase in how it is experienced or perceived by subjects (Weber, 1834; Fechner, 1860). Experiment 3 provides an example experimental design.

EXPERIMENT 3: Suppose that we present subjects with two weights and ask them to identify which is heavier. One weight has a mass of x kg and the other has a mass of $x + y$ kg. We repeat this for different values of x and y. We pay particular attention to the smallest values of y where subjects can accurately identify the heavier of the two. Suppose that, for every x, we identify the smallest value of y where subjects can just accurately identify the heavier of the weights.

An experimental regularity is that the y where subjects can just accurately identify the heavier of the weights is increasing in x. In fact, there can appear to be a linear relationship between this threshold y and the corresponding x.

---

[14] Summerfield and Tsetsos (2012) describe perceptual choice designs as those where "observers detect, discriminate, and categorize noisy sensory information."

[15] Summerfield and Tsetsos (2012) describe economic choice designs as those that "employ stimuli that are perceptually unambiguous, often in the visual domain" and subjects "chose among different options on the basis of their associated reinforcement history." The authors cite a multiarmed bandit experiment as an example of an economic choice design. The term economic decision can also refer to a serial choice task involving known items (often snack foods) that occur after willingness to pay elicitations have been made (for example, Oud et al., 2016).

Somewhat more generally, we denote φ as the physical intensity of a stimulus and $\Delta\varphi$ as the smallest change in the stimulus intensity required to be noticeable by subjects. This $\Delta\varphi$ is sometimes referred to as the *just noticeable difference*. The linear relationship between the just noticeable difference and the stimulus intensity is known as *Weber's law*:

$$\Delta\varphi = c\varphi,$$

where c is a constant.[16]

Fechner's Law

In an effort to relate physical stimuli to how they are perceived by a subject, Fechner (1860) sought the implications of Weber's law. If sensation is constant within the just noticeable differences ($\Delta\varphi$) and if Weber's law is descriptively correct, then an expression could be obtained that relates the intensity of a stimulus to the sensation of that stimulus. Specifically, Fechner argued that these assumptions imply that increases in the stimulus intensity cause logarithmic increases in the sensation of that intensity. If we denote the physical intensity of a stimulus as φ and its perceived intensity as ψ, then *Fechner's law* describes their relationship as follows:

$$\psi = k * \log \varphi,$$

where k is a constant.[17]

Note that Fechner's law implies a diminishing sensitivity to all stimuli, including economic stimuli. For example, the xth dollar will be perceived as more intense than the yth dollar, where $x < y$. In the following, we describe the modern notion of utility. We also note that more than 100 years before Fechner, Bernoulli (1738) proposed a logarithmic specification for the utility of money.

However, despite the strong assumptions and the apparent violations of Weber's law[18] (from which Fechner's law is derived), Fechner's law was largely considered to be the best characterization of the relationship between stimulus and sensation for about 100 years (Stevens, 1961; Gescheider, 1997).

---

[16] Despite the use of the term *law*, the expression seems to not hold for all values, particularly low stimulus values. See Gescheider (1997, ch. 1) for evidence of a nonlinear relationship for low values and Solomon (2009) for evidence of a nonmonotonic relationship for very small values.

[17] See Murray (1993) for more on the background of Fechner's law.

[18] See Gescheider (1997, ch. 1) for classic evidence that sensation is not necessarily constant within just noticeable differences.

The Range of Psychophysics Experimental Designs

Until now, we have confined attention to experimental designs where subjects are simultaneously presented with two stimuli and are directed to perform a judgment on their intensity. Another example of this *discrimination* design is: here are two gray disks – indicate which is darker (Figure 4a).

However, this is only one of the many possible experimental designs. Instead of selecting between stimuli, the subject might be directed to reproduce a stimulus. An example of this *reproduction* design is: here is a gray disk that will disappear – reproduce its appearance on this gray disk with an adjustable darkness (Figure 4b).[19]

Another production task would be to find a partition such that an adjustable stimulus appears midway between two different stimuli. An example of this *bisection* design is: here is a light gray disk, a dark gray disk, and a gray disk of adjustable darkness – adjust the appearance of the disk so that it appears to make two equal darkness intervals (Figure 4c).[20]

These are just three of a very large number of psychophysics experimental designs. Recall the instances where you confidently detected a vibrating phone in your pocket, only to later discover that your phone did not actually vibrate. In *detection* experiments, subjects might be presented with a very weak stimulus intensity on some trials, no stimulus on other trials, and on every trial subjects are asked if they detected a stimulus.[21,22] Furthermore, the stimuli might be presented sequentially, rather than simultaneously, as would seem appropriate for judgments of temporal duration or sound.

Ratio estimation designs present subjects with two stimuli and direct subjects to estimate the ratio of their intensity.[23] Other *magnitude estimation* designs might assign a numerical magnitude to one stimulus and direct subjects to estimate the numerical magnitude of another stimulus.[24] A variation of this

---

[19] See Hollingworth (1910), Huttenlocher, Hedges, and Vevea (2000), Allred et al. (2016), and Duffy and Smith (2020) for examples of reproduction experimental designs.

[20] Plateau (1872) is often credited for pioneering the bisection design. See Munsell, Sloan, and Godlove (1933) for a later contribution and brief review of the early literature. *Bisection* refers to designs where subjects partition the stimuli into two equal regions, whereas *equisection* refers to analogous designs where subjects partition the stimuli into a larger number of equal regions.

[21] See Gescheider, Wright, and Polak (1971) for an example of a detection experiment.

[22] In the stimuli that we consider, the terms detection and discrimination can be used unambiguously: in detection designs, the null stimulus is a choice object, and in discrimination designs, none of the choice objects are the null stimulus. However, see Kingdom and Prins (2016, ch. 2) for a discussion of these terms with more exotic designs.

[23] For example, Engen and Tulunay (1957) direct subjects to judge whether a weight is more than half or less than half as heavy as another weight.

[24] For example, Stevens (1956).

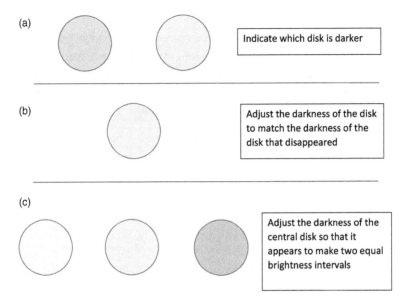

Figure 4 Three examples of different psychophysics experimental designs. Panel (a) depicts a *discrimination* experiment where the subject is directed to select which of the disks appears to be darker. Panel (b) depicts a *reproduction* experiment where the subject is directed to reproduce the darkness of a disk that was shown to the subject but not visible during the reproduction. Panel (c) depicts a *bisection* experiment where the subject is directed to adjust the darkness of the middle disk so that its darkness appears to be halfway between the light and dark disks.

design is to let subjects select the numerical magnitudes for both stimuli or not assign a number to a baseline.[25]

Still other *ratio production* designs might present subjects with a target stimulus and direct them to adjust another stimulus to be some ratio (say, a third as intense) of the target.[26] Finally, *magnitude production* designs might assign a numerical magnitude and direct the subject to adjust a stimulus until it matches their sensation.[27] See Gescheider (1997, ch. 11) for more on these estimation and production tasks. See Kingdom and Prins (2016, ch. 3) and Wichmann and Jäkel (2018) for recent overviews of the experimental designs.

Psychophysics experiments have been conducted on a staggeringly large number of stimulus types, including heaviness, smell, taste, temperature,

---

[25] Stevens (1971) argues that this is the preferred design.
[26] See Churcher (1935) for an early example.   [27] For example, Stevens and Guirao (1962).

pressure on the skin, frequency of vibrations applied to the skin, amplitude of vibrations applied to the skin, and even the strength of electrical shocks.[28] See Laming (1986) for an impressive collection of stimulus types. However, perhaps most relevant to experimental economists, the investigated stimuli include judgments of loudness, brightness, distance, length, area, temporal duration, and numerosity.

Stevens' Law

When we plot the results of Experiment 4, the relationship between stimulus and sensation seems to not follow a logarithmic specification. Evidence suggests that it follows a power specification (Stevens, 1936).

EXPERIMENT 4: Consider a design where we direct subjects to listen to a tone with a certain objectively measurable loudness. We subsequently offer the subjects a tone with adjustable loudness and direct them to adjust the loudness so that it seems to be half as loud as the first tone.

Evidence subsequently accumulated (Stevens, 1957, 1960, 1961), which supported the claim that the relationship between stimulus and sensation follows the power law, with different stimuli exhibiting different sensitivities. What has become known as *Stevens' law* is[29]:

$$\psi = k * \varphi^{\alpha},$$

where k is a constant and exponent α depends on the stimulus type.

When plotted on log–log axes, functions that follow a power law are linear with the slope of the exponent. See Figure 5 for the results of experiments of brightness, apparent length, and electric shock.

While Stevens' law purports a relationship between stimulus magnitude and perception that depends on the stimulus type, we note that when $\alpha < 1$, there will be diminishing sensitivity to increases in the stimuli. Relatedly, in discussing what is now known as the Saint Petersburg paradox, Bernoulli (1738) notes that a colleague named Cramer speculated that utility for money might have a square root specification; in other words, a power function with an exponent of 0.5.

---

[28] We suspect that few current Institutional Review Boards would permit administering electrical shocks to subjects.

[29] See Stevens (1961) and Murray (1993) for more on the history of the power law specification of sensation before Stevens.

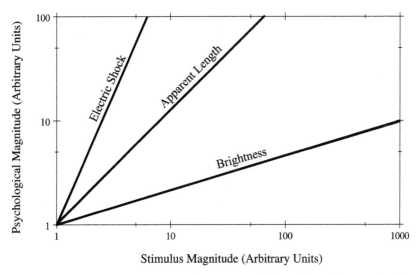

Figure 5 The relationship between stimulus magnitude and how it is perceived by subjects is plotted in log–log coordinates. The slope of each line is the exponent of the power function governing the growth of the psychological magnitude. Electric shock refers to a 60 Hertz current applied to the finger. Apparent length refers to judgments of the lengths of lines. Brightness refers to judgments of brightness of white light. This figure is based on figure 3 in Stevens (1960).

The Elusive Quest for a Single Equation

Despite the success of Stevens' law, concerns emerged about the elicitation methods (Anderson, 1970; Shepard, 1981).[30] Eventually, it became clear that Weber's law, Fechner's law, and Stevens' law each had significant problems. Subsequently, Krueger (1989) and Murray (1993) noted the difficulties in finding a single equation to relate stimuli and sensation, and, recently, Wichmann and Jäkel (2018) described these efforts as "elusive." Nonetheless, Weber, Fechner, and Stevens made significant contributions to understanding how stimuli are perceived and these references continue to appear in the literature. On the other hand, economists can likely sympathize with the difficulty in finding a single equation relating (economic) stimuli to sensation.

Stochastic Responses and the Psychometric Function

Consider an experiment where subjects are presented with two objects and asked to identify which is longer (see Experiment 5). The responses are stochastic in that a subject, given the same pair of objects, could give different

---

[30] See Bernasconi and Seri (2016) for a more recent reference noting many of the criticisms.

responses on different trials. However, there is a relationship between the difference in the lengths and the probability of a correct response. Thurstone (1927a, 1927b) is credited for providing the first explicit account for noise in the imperfect judgments of detecting the more intense stimuli.

Because the psychophysics experimenter knows the objective measures of the stimuli and can make small changes in the intensity of the stimuli, the experimenter can deduce the relationship between features of the stimuli and the response. The *psychometric function* can refer to a characterization of the relationship between the response and the objective features of the stimuli.[31] In discrimination experiments, psychometric functions will often characterize the relationship between response and the difference in the stimuli. In detection experiments, psychometric functions will often characterize the relationship between the response and the strength of the (non-null) stimuli.[32]

EXPERIMENT 5: Suppose subjects were presented with two objects – one with a length of 3 cm and another object with a length different from 3 cm. Some of these objects are longer than 3 cm and others are shorter than 3 cm. The subjects are asked to identify which object is longer. In one treatment, subjects make visual judgments. In another treatment, subjects make haptic (touch) judgments.

See Figure 6 for the psychometric function from Experiment 5. We note that the psychometric function characterizes the feature that small changes in the stimuli lead to gradual (not sudden) changes in the responses. We also note that this psychometric function suggests that vision judgments are more accurate than haptic judgments because the psychometric function of the former is steeper than the psychometric function of the latter.

Signal Detection Theory

Although the perception of objective stimuli is imperfect, subjects are not passive observers in the process. While subjects receive noisy signals about the stimuli, subjects strive to interpret the signals and make an optimal response,

[31] See Kingdom and Prins (2016, ch. 4) for various specifications of the psychometric function and Gescheider (1997, ch. 4) for theoretical background on the psychometric function.

[32] The behavioral or experimental economist likely has a psychometric function on their shelf. Figure 2 in Luce (1959, ch. 2) depicts a psychometric function that characterizes choice in a discrimination experiment as a function of the differences in stimuli. However, we note that Luce does not use the term *psychometric function*. Mosteller and Nogee (1951) also depict several smooth relationships between economic choice and economic stimuli, as measured by estimated expected utility. We also note that Mosteller and Nogee (1951) does not use the term *psychometric function*.

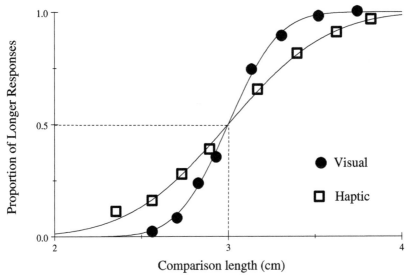

Figure 6 Psychometric functions from Experiment 5 where subjects determine whether an object with 3 cm of length is longer than an object with length different from 3 cm. The subjects perform this by visual judgment or by haptic (touch) judgment. Note that the psychometric functions, for both visual and haptic judgments, at 3 cm suggest that lines slightly longer or shorter than 3 cm would be judged to be longer with a probability close to 0.5. Also note that the visual judgments appear to be more accurate than haptic judgments. In fact, the visual judgments appear to second-order stochastically dominate the haptic judgments, in that the means are identical but there is less noise in the former. This figure is based on figure 7.1B in Wichmann and Jäkel (2018).

given the features of the setting. Signal detection theory[33] is possibly the most successful model to describe this process. For an experimental economist, perhaps the most notable implication is that changing the relative material incentives for various choices can affect responses in otherwise identical perceptual judgments.

Consider a judgment of the lengths of two lines. The line on the left has objective length x_L and the line on the right has objective length x_R. One way to model the imperfect perception of lengths is to assume additive noise. For example, the perceived length of the left line is $x_L + \varepsilon_L$ and the perceived length of the right line is $x_R + \varepsilon_R$, where both ε_L and ε_R are drawn from a distribution with a mean of zero. According to this specification, given the trial-specific

---

[33] For more on signal detection theory, see Gescheider (1997, ch. 5–8), Hautus, Macmillan, and Creelman (2022), and Woodford (2020).

draws e_L and e_R, the subject perceives the left line to be longer if and only if $x_L + e_L > x_R + e_R$. However, the judgment is likely to be affected by details of the environment.

Similar to experiments described above, we provide an example of a design where subjects are asked to judge lines lengths. However, in Experiment 6, there are two different material incentives treatments.

EXPERIMENT 6: Suppose that we direct subjects to judge the lengths of the lines on the right and left. In one treatment, we give the following instructions: "Is the left line longer than the right line? Answer 'yes' or 'no.' A correct response will earn $10. An incorrect response will earn $0." In another treatment, we give the following instructions: "Is the left line longer than the right line? Answer 'yes' or 'no.' A correct 'yes' will earn $15 and a correct 'no' will earn $5. An incorrect response will earn $0."

Even though the perceptual questions are identical, we expect more "yes" responses in the second treatment than the first treatment.[34] Note that the incentives in the first treatment regard the responses symmetrically, but the incentives in the second treatment do not regard the responses symmetrically. Suppose that the subject judges the right line to be slightly longer than the left line and accounts for the fact that their perception is noisy. In the first treatment, the subject will respond "no" because it maximizes their expected utility. However, there are values where the subject will respond "yes" in the second treatment – even if they deem the right line to be longer – because that response maximizes their expected utility.

Below we have a line judgment experiment, analogous to the design in Experiment 6. However, in Experiment 7, we have treatments based on the position of the correct response.

EXPERIMENT 7: Suppose that we direct subjects to judge the lengths of the lines on the right and left. In one treatment, 90 percent of the trials have the longest line on the left and 10 percent of the trials have the longest line on the right. In another treatment, 10 percent of the trials have the longest line on the left and 90 percent of the trials have the longest line on the right. Subjects are informed of the distributions. Both treatments are given the following instructions: "Is the left line longer than the right line? Answer 'yes' or 'no.' A correct response will earn $10. An incorrect response will earn $0."

---

[34] For example, see Swets, Tanner, and Birdsall (1961) and See et al. (1997).

In Experiment 7, again, the perceptual questions are identical. However, for any given pair of lines, we expect more "yes" responses in the first treatment than the second treatment.[35] Consider, again, a subject who judges the right line to be slightly longer than the left line and accounts for the fact that their perception is noisy. Subjects will strive to combine the information contained in their idiosyncratic perceptions with their knowledge of the distribution of lines.

In the second treatment, the subject will respond "no" because the right is judged longer and the longest lines are on the right. However, there are values where the subject will respond "yes" in the first treatment – even if the right line is perceived to be slightly longer. This is because there is a higher probability that their perception was a mistake because the longest lines are on the left.

The signal detection theory offers a model consistent with these observations, where subjects strive to make optimal use of the features of the setting. In Experiments 6 and 7, this corresponds (respectively) to using the different material incentives and different distributions to strive to make the optimal response.

Nonchoice Data

Finally, in addition to simply observing the subject response, the experimenter can also observe nonchoice data, which can provide additional clues about the deliberation. For example, response times have been used to make sense of the responses in psychophysics experiments. Early research found that longer response times are associated with judgments closer to indifference (Henmon, 1911; Volkmann, 1934) and that suboptimal perceptual judgments tend to have longer response times than optimal perceptual judgments (Henmon, 1911; Kellogg, 1931). Subsequently, researchers have sought to make sense of these (and other) regularities (Luce and Green, 1972; Ratcliff and Rouder, 1998) in developing models that specify a joint distribution over choice and response times.[36]

Key Psychophysics Insights for Experimental Economists

While a more thorough discussion of the history of thought in psychophysics is beyond the scope of this Element, we now summarize some of the key insights for experimental economists:

- The psychophysics experimenter knows the objectively measurable properties of both the stimuli and the responses.

---

[35] See Tanner, Swets, and Green (1956) for a classic reference.
[36] For example, the drift diffusion models that we describe in Section 4.

- This technique can generate stochastic responses that tend to more accurately identify the more intense stimulus when the stimuli become less similar.
- The subjects are not passive recipients of the stochastic sensory information but rather strive to interpret the signals and make an optimal response, given the features of the setting.
- The use of nonchoice data can provide clues about the deliberation process.
- Longer response times tend to be associated with decisions that are closer to indifference.

3 Psychophysics Insights Already in the Economics Literature

Stochastic Choice and Classic Psychophysics References

Both theoretical models of stochastic choice due to imprecise preferences or efforts to interpret apparently random choice data have been motivated by the classic psychophysics literature. For example, Luce (1959), Becker, DeGroot, and Marschak (1963), Hildenbrand (1971), McFadden (1974, 2001), Machina (1985), Mas-Colell, Whinston, and Green (1995), Ballinger and Wilcox (1997), Loomis et al. (1998), Butler (2000), Butler and Loomes (2007), Blavatskyy (2008, 2011), Bordalo, Gennaioli, and Shleifer (2012), Lévy-Garboua et al. (2012), Fudenberg, Iijima, and Strzalecki (2015), Navarro-Martinez et al. (2018), Alós-Ferrer, Fehr, and Netzer (2021), Khaw, Li, and Woodford (2021), and Horan, Manzini, and Mariotti (2022) have cited Weber, Fechner, or Thurstone.

Individual Choice without (External) Uncertainty

Despite this strong connection between the classic psychophysics references and models of stochastic choice, psychophysics has been present in other economics topics. For example, early motivations for utility and justifications for decreasing marginal utility made reference to the insights of Weber and Fechner, which were then state-of-the-art science.[37] While subsequent economics researchers sought to eliminate the psychological underpinnings of utility theory, it can seem difficult to justify the general assumption of diminishing marginal utility (ranging from possessions as varied as wealth, hamburgers, pet scorpions, bathrooms in one's residence, etc.) without an appeal to the tendency of diminishing sensitivity to stimuli found by Weber and Fechner.

Researchers have also employed the Stevens' power law in order to better understand the perception of temporal duration (Antonides, Verhoef, and Van

---

[37] See Bruni and Sugden (2007) for a somewhat recent account and see Stigler (1950a, 1950b) for a classic account.

Aalst, 2002; Brocas, Carrillo, and Tarrasó, 2018), the perception of various time periods in delay discounting problems (Zauberman et al., 2009), the perception of inflation (Antonides, 2008), and to better understand elicited measures of health (Salomon and Murray, 2004).

Even when the original formulation of a result did not explicitly acknowledge psychophysics insights, the insights can be nonetheless present. Consider the well-known effect that people might be often willing to bear an inconvenience to save an amount (say $5) on a smaller purchase but are unwilling to bear the same inconvenience to save the same amount on a larger purchase. The first version of this is often attributed to Savage (1954). Perhaps, the most well-known version appears in Tversky and Kahneman (1981, Problem 10).[38] It seems that consumers *feel* that the difference between $10 and $15 is more intense than the difference between $120 and $125. Despite the basis for this in the classic psychophysics literature, it was apparently not pointed out until Thaler (1980).[39]

Also, consider the experimental result that the inclusion of a dominated element in a choice set can often increase the likelihood that the dominating element is selected (Huber, Payne, and Puto, 1982). This behavior is consistent neither with classic models of choice nor with random utility models. However, Natenzon (2019) proposes that subjects have an imperfect perception of their preferences (Thurstone, 1927a, 1927b) and the addition of the dominated item differentially affects the evaluation of the other elements of the choice set in a way that renders the dominating element more attractive.

Psychophysics insights have also been used to justify *textbook* economics assumptions other than diminishing marginal utility. Argenziano and Gilboa (2017) show that Weber's law and an independence assumption imply Cobb–Douglass preferences, where the decision-maker cannot distinguish between units within the just-noticeable differences.

Individual Choice with (External) Uncertainty

Likewise, psychophysical insights have been used to better understand concepts that were not explicitly motivated by psychophysical insights. For example, Rabin (2000) argues that small stakes risk aversion coupled with the

---

[38] The item, designed to rule out several potential objections, is phrased as follows: "Imagine that you are about to purchase a jacket for $125 (resp. $15) and a calculator for $15 (resp. $125). The calculator salesman informs you that the calculator you wish to buy is on sale for $10 (resp. $120) at the other branch of the store, located 20 minutes drive away. Would you make the trip to the other store?" The authors report that 68 percent of respondents would make the drive to save $5 on the $15 calculator purchase, but only 29 percent would do so for the $125 calculator purchase.

[39] Further, this effect has been used to explain the apparent effect of greater price dispersion for goods that have larger mean prices. For example, see Pratt, Wise, and Zeckhauser (1979).

diminishing marginal utility of wealth can yield absurd implications. For example, consider an expected utility maximizing subject who turns down a 50–50 gamble with a loss of $100 and a gain of $110, for any initial wealth level. Diminishing marginal utility of wealth implies that the decision-maker will also reject a 50–50 gamble with a loss of $1000 and a gain of any amount of money, no matter how large. A common explanation for these results is *loss aversion*: subjects are more sensitive to losses (events that reduce wealth below a reference level) than they are to gains (events that increase wealth above the reference level).[40]

Khaw, Li, and Woodford (2021) offer another explanation for the results of Rabin (2000). The authors propose a model where the objectively specified payments in the choice are subject to imperfect mental representations that are encoded logarithmically (Fechner, 1860). The authors argue that the model generates the behavior identified by Rabin, even without assuming that the subjects have a diminishing marginal utility of money.

Relatedly, Frydman and Jin (2022) propose a model where an agent selects between a certain payoff and a gamble, where the monetary payoffs are imperfectly perceived. Due to processing constraints of the agent, values that have been frequently encountered are perceived with greater precision than values that have not been frequently encountered. The authors then conduct experiments where subjects decide between certain payoffs and gambles, where the distribution of the values varies.[41] In one experiment, the values are drawn from two distributions: one with more variance than the other. The authors find that risky choice is noisier in the high-variance treatment than the low-variance treatment. In another experiment, the subjects are given piecewise uniform distributions, where one region is much more likely than the other region; in one treatment, the unlikely region in the upper range of numbers and, in the other treatment, the unlikely region in the lower range of numbers. The authors find that the subjects are more risk seeking in the higher likelihood regions than the lower likelihood regions. In other words, a risky choice can depend on the environment because the values are imperfectly perceived.

Economic data has also been used to show evidence of gradual psychometric-type results in choice. Alós-Ferrer and Garagnani (2021), using data from previously published papers, note a positive relationship between the probability of selecting the estimated optimal gamble with the estimated difference in the expected utilities of the gambles. Alós-Ferrer and Garagnani (2022a) describe a computerized card game where the optimal choice depends on the

---

[40] See Rabin (2000) for the initial explanation and see Wakker (2010, ch. 8) for more on the explanation within the loss aversion literature.

[41] In Section 5, we discuss the perceptual experiment in Frydman and Jin (2022).

risk preferences of the subjects. The authors find that choice frequencies are related to differences in the estimated expected utilities of the choices. The authors also report a negative relationship between the absolute differences in the estimated expected utilities and the response times of the decision. In both papers, the authors attribute their results to the imperfect perception of (economic) stimuli, analogous to the insights of Fechner and Thurstone.

In expected utility theory, the probabilities linearly map into the representation.[42] For example, consider a gamble with two outcomes: Events 1 and 2. Event 1 occurs with probability p_1 and will give the decision-maker utility U_1. Event 2 occurs with probability p_2 and will give the decision-maker utility U_2. The expected utility of this gamble is:

$$EU = p_1 U_1 + p_2 U_2.$$

One of the primary ways that prospect theory deviates from the expected utility theory is that the probabilities do not linearly enter into the representation. Rather, the prospect theory posits a nonlinear probability weighting function $w(p)$ (Kahneman and Tversky, 1979). Considerable attention has been devoted to understanding the shape of this probability weighting function.[43] Prelec (1998) proposes a probability weighting function of:

$$w(p) = \exp\left(-(-\ln p)^{\alpha}\right) \text{ for } 0 < \alpha < 1.$$

Takahashi (2011) argues that the shape of the Prelec's specification can be understood by an appeal to the classic psychophysics insights of Weber and Stevens.[44]

Choice in Strategic Settings

While our discussion has been confined to individual choice, one can also find psychophysics insights in the study of strategic interactions or behavior in games.

For example, petroleum engineers noticed that winning bidders in oil tract auctions tended to receive very low returns on their investments (Capen, Clapp, and Campbell, 1971). These are *common value auctions*, in that it might be reasonable to assume that each bidder values the tract the

---

[42] For example, see Mas-Colell, Whinston, and Green (1995, ch. 6).

[43] For example, Tversky and Kahneman (1992), Camerer and Ho (1994), Prelec (1998), and Gonzalez and Wu (1999). For a visualization of the Prelec specification and other probability weighting functions for various parameter values, see https://olivierlharidon.shinyapps.io/probability_weighting_functions/

[44] Also note that Sinn (1985) shows that Weber's law implies constant relative risk aversion for a myopic expected utility maximizer.

same. However, each bidder has a different estimate of the value of the tract.[45] If the bids in such common value settings are a function only of the bidder-specific estimates, the winning bidder also had the highest estimate (and each of the other bidders had lower estimates). Note that the maximum of the estimates is not an accurate estimate of the true value. Therefore, if bidders only bid as a function of their estimate, they will bid with a biased estimate of the value of the object. This overbidding has become known as the *Winner's Curse* (Thaler, 1988).[46] In order to avoid the Winner's Curse, bids in common value auctions need to be a function of both the bidder-specific estimates, and if they win the auction, then every other bidder has a lower estimate.

In order to study the Winner's Curse in the laboratory, experimenters need to produce an object that is equally valued by subjects, but subjects would have imperfect estimates of its value. Early experiments auctioned jars of an unknown number of coins and found that even MBA student subjects exhibited the Winner's Curse (Bazerman and Samuelson, 1983).[47] The precise value of the jar is known to the experimenter but imperfectly perceived by the subjects. It is imperfect perception, coupled with insufficiently accounting for this imprecision in their bid, which leads to the Winner's Curse. It is obviously quite valuable to the experimenter to know the objective value of the object being auctioned.[48]

Furthermore, recall the psychometric function, which characterizes the smooth relationship between behavior and objective stimuli in psychophysics experiments. Experimental evidence also suggests a smooth relationship between behavior in games and the stimuli of the payoffs. For example, Heinemann, Nagel, and Ockenfels (2009) study binary-action N-player coordination games. Subjects decide between actions A and B. Action A guarantees a payoff of X (where X ranges from €1.5 to €15). Action B pays €15 if a sufficient number of subjects also play B; otherwise, it pays 0. Figure 7 depicts the smooth relationship between the proportion of B actions and X (the payoff from action A).

Just as the choice among stimuli is stochastic, choice in a strategic setting can be analogously stochastic. McKelvey and Palfrey (1995) define a *quantal response equilibrium* (QRE) to be the fixed-point of noisy best response

---

[45] These differences in estimates of the value might arise from each bidder performing independent tests in order to estimate the available oil in the tract.

[46] In fact, Mead, Moseidjord, and Sorensen (1983) present evidence that some bidders in oil tract auctions earn negative returns. These outcomes are consistent with bids larger than the value of the tract.

[47] A countless number of game theory instructors have subsequently auctioned such jars in their classes.

[48] See Krishna (2002, ch. 6) for a discussion of more general common value auction setting.

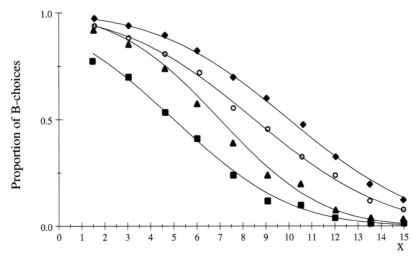

Figure 7 Depiction of the smooth relationship between the sure payoff of
X and choice in coordination games across game treatments. The
coordination threshold is the fraction of *B* choices required for the €15
payment, and this varied across treatments. Diamonds, triangles, and squares
refer (respectively) to coordination thresholds of 1/3, 2/3, and 1. The open
circles refer to the lottery treatment where *B* would pay €15 with probability
2/3. Note that all four treatments have a smooth downward relationship as
X increases. This figure is based on figure 3 in Heinemann, Nagel, and
Ockenfels (2009).

functions. This is the extension of individual stochastic choice to multiple
players in a strategic setting.

First, let us start with the tractable Luce (1959) logit specification of individual stochastic choice.[49] Suppose that the decision-maker has a binary choice[50]
of *U*, with a payoff of π_U, and a choice of *D*, with a payoff of π_D. In this
specification, the probability that the decision-maker selects *U* depends on the
payoff of *U*, the payoff of *D*, and a logit precision parameter λ:

$$\Pr(U) = \exp(\lambda\pi_U)/[\exp(\lambda\pi_U) + \exp(\lambda\pi_D)].$$

Note that as λ converges to ∞, the probability that the choice with the
higher payoff is selected converges to 1. Also note that as λ converges to
0, the probability that the choice with the higher payoff is selected
converges to 0.5.

---

[49] As mentioned earlier, Luce (1959) was motivated by classic psychophysics research.
[50] This can be generalized to an arbitrary number of choice options.

Furthermore, the analogous expression would hold for another individual decision-maker with a binary choice of L (with payoff π_L) and R (with payoff π_R):

$$\Pr(R) = \exp(\lambda\pi_R)/[\exp(\lambda\pi_R) + \exp(\lambda\pi_L)].$$

McKelvey and Palfrey (1995) extend these individual stochastic choice specifications to the analogous logit equilibrium for strategic settings. Notably, this QRE implies smooth (not "step-function") best response curves and has successes explaining the experimental data.

To illustrate QRE and distinguish its predictions from those of Nash equilibria, consider the generalized matching pennies games in Table 1.[51]

Observe that, regardless of the value of X, there are neither dominant strategies nor pure strategy Nash equilibria. However, there is a unique mixed strategy Nash equilibrium, which varies according to X. For each value of X, the mixed strategy Nash equilibrium is that $\Pr(U) = 0.5$. For X equal to 1, 4, and 5, the mixed strategy Nash equilibrium is $\Pr(R)$ (respectively) equal to 0.5, 0.8, and 0.9. In Figure 8, these are labeled as (respectively) as N1, N4, and N9. In other words, the Nash equilibrium predicts that changes in X affect $\Pr(R)$ but will not affect $\Pr(U)$.

The QRE entails the pair of $\Pr(U)$ and $\Pr(R)$, which solve:

$$\Pr(U) = \exp(\lambda X(1 - \Pr(R)))/[\exp(\lambda X(1 - \Pr(R))) + \exp(\lambda\Pr(R))].$$

$$\Pr(R) = \exp(\lambda(1 - \Pr(U)))/[\exp(\lambda(1 - \Pr(U))) + \exp(\lambda\Pr(U))].$$

We note that when λ converges to ∞, the predictions of QRE converge to those of the Nash equilibrium. However, for smaller values of λ, QRE predicts that X will affect both $\Pr(R)$ and $\Pr(U)$. Figure 8 shows the standard Nash equilibrium predictions with the corresponding step-function best response functions

Table 1 Generalized
matching pennies where X is
1, 4, or 9 (Ochs, 1995)

		Column	
		L	R
Row	U	$X, 0$	$0, 1$
	D	$0, 1$	$1, 0$

---

[51] See Goeree, Holt, and Palfrey (2010).

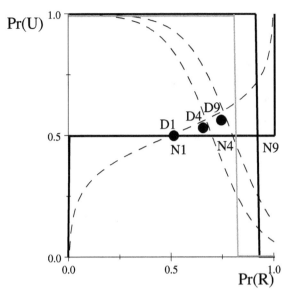

Figure 8 Best response relationships in generalized matching pennies games.
The standard, sudden ("step-function") best response correspondences
are in bold. The (smooth) logit best response curves are dashed.
Row's standard best response function for $X = 1$ is omitted from the figure.
The labels N1, N4, and N9 indicate the Nash equilibria of the games,
where X is (respectively) 1, 4, and 9. Note that each of the Nash equilibrium
predictions is such that $\Pr(U) = 0.5$. The labels D1, D4, and D9 indicate the
(respective) experimental observations from Ochs (1995). Note that
only the payoffs of Row vary across treatments. Despite this, the data
(and broadly consistent with the QRE predictions) suggest that both Row and
Column player mixtures will be affected by X. This figure is based on
figure 1 in Goeree, Holt, and Palfrey (2003).

depicted in bold. The figure also shows the smooth QRE best response functions, which are dashed. Furthermore, the figure shows the experimental observations labeled as D1, D4, and D5.

Unlike the predictions of the Nash equilibrium, QRE can accommodate the intuitive prediction that changes in X will affect the mixtures of both Row and Column players. This is an example of a concept, initially motivated by the classic psychophysics literature, which contributes to our understanding of behavior in games.

In summary, while psychophysics insights are perhaps not known by many economists, these insights are indeed present in economics.

4 Models that are Difficult to Test without Psychophysics Experimental Techniques

Some models make claims that are difficult to test with standard experimental economics data. This difficulty largely stems from the fact that the objective valuations are not observable to the experimenter. However, when the experimenter can observe the objectively optimal choice, these models can be scrutinized. In this section, we describe some models that are most appropriately tested by experiments that use psychophysics techniques.

Models of Rational Inattention

For example, rational inattention models posit that the decision-maker is faced with external uncertainty about the state of the world. However, the decision-maker can reduce the uncertainty via a costly process of paying attention to and processing relevant information. Therefore, the decision regarding how much information to attend to before making the decision is a key component of the models. See, for example, Sims (2003), Caplin and Dean (2015), and Matějka and McKay (2015).

Rational inattention models contain a latent cost-of-attention function that guides the decision on how much information to attend to. Specifically, the decision-maker has prior beliefs about the state of the world and decides how much information to pay attention to; this informs the posterior beliefs, and the optimal decision is made based on these posterior beliefs. See Maćkowiak, Matějka, and Wiederholt (2023) for a recent overview of the literature.

For example, rational inattention models predict that choice is stochastic, that decision-makers will pay more attention to volatile information, and that increasing the material incentives will induce more attention.

Rational intention models can offer intuitively appealing explanations to behavior that is difficult to explain with random utility models. For example, rational inattention models can account for violations of *monotonicity*, where an element b is selected from a set $\{a,b\}$ less frequently than from a set $\{a,b,c\}$. Rational attention can account for this occurrence because the inclusion of element c can change the choice of attention in a way that favors b.

Another intuitively appealing explanation involves the problem of duplicates when applied to the Luce (1959) random choice model.[52] Consider a decision-maker who is given the choice between the bus and a train and selects both with

---

[52] A similar argument was first made by Debreu (1960). See Matějka and McKay (2015) for more on this random inattention resolution to the red bus, blue bus problem.

probability 0.5. Now we offer the decision-maker a choice among a red bus, a blue bus, and a train. The Luce (1959) random choice model would predict each with probability 1/3. However, a rationally inattentive decision-maker would not incur costs to distinguish between the busses. As a result, the decision-maker would select the train with probability 0.5 and both buses with probability 0.25.

Rational inattention has been used to better understand behavior in numerous economic settings.[53] However, the nature of this latent cost function can be difficult to characterize unless the experimenter knows all of the objective features of the environment.

Drift Diffusion Models

A different class of decision models, referred to as drift diffusion model (DDM), conceptualizes a binary choice where an agent accumulates evidence or engages in memory retrieval.[54] This process generates a random drift and the agent makes a decision for one of the options when the random variable hits a decision boundary.[55] Therefore, DDMs make predictions over both the stochastic nature of choice and distributions of response times.

A way to formalize the decision between A and B is that Z_t represents the information that the decision-maker receives over time. If B_t is Brownian motion and δ is the drift rate, then one specification is: $Z_t = \delta t + B_t$. Note that in this specification, $B_0 = 0$. If $\delta > 0$, then A is the correct decision and if $\delta < 0$, then B is the correct decision.

The process continues until Z_t hits a decision boundary. The decision-maker stops if $Z_t \geq b^A{}_t$ and selects A. The decision-maker stops if $Z_t \leq b^B{}_t$ and selects B.

As an example, consider Figure 9, which depicts a DDM for an agent deciding between A and B. There is a drift toward the option with the larger utility (A), but both options are selected with some probability. In our figure, the decision boundaries are constant and symmetric, although this need not be

---

[53] A very small sample of the applications includes business cycle dynamics (Maćkowiak and Mirko, 2015), price setting (Maćkowiak and Wiederholt, 2009; Stevens, 2020), hiring decisions (Acharya and Wee, 2020), reaction to taxes (Taubinsky and Rees-Jones, 2018), the home bias effect (Mondria and Wu, 2010), patterns in technology adoption (Naeher, 2022), political polarization (Yuksel, 2022), and coordination (Dessein, Galeotti, and Santos, 2016).

[54] While there are differences between rational inattention models and DDMs, we note that both specify that the decision-maker arrives at a choice only after sufficient information acquisition or confidence in the choice. However, a more complete discussion of the relationship between rational inattention models and DDMs is beyond the scope of this Element. It also seems to be the case that there is not an overview comparing and contrasting these sets of models.

[55] For example, see Ratcliff (1978) and Ratcliff and McKoon (2008). See Evans and Wagenmakers (2020) for a recent overview of what has become a very large literature.

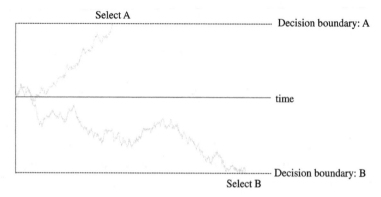

Figure 9 Depiction of two possible trajectories in a baseline DDM, with symmetric and constant decision boundaries. The trajectory of the choice of *A* has a relatively short response time and the trajectory of the choice of *B* has a relatively long response time. Here, the decision boundaries are constant and symmetric, but many DDMs posit nonconstant or nonsymmetric decision boundaries.

the case. Figure 9 depicts two different trajectories: a choice of *A* with a relatively short response time and a choice of *B* with a relatively long response time.

For example, Ratcliff (2014) examines the results from several discrimination perceptual judgment tasks, which also include response time data. The author estimates the drift rates consistent with a model of constant but nonsymmetric decision boundaries. These estimates of drift rates are similar to the normalized measures of accuracy in the tasks.

Fudenberg, Strack, and Strzalecki (2018) propose a DDM describing a decision-maker with a choice involving uncertain utilities, and there is a cost of gathering information about the choice problem. Unlike the depiction in Figure 9, Fudenberg, Strack, and Strzalecki do not assume constant decision boundaries. In fact, in this setting, it is optimal that the decision boundaries collapse. An implication of these decision boundaries is that suboptimal decisions will have longer response times than optimal decisions.

Suppose that *A* is the optimal choice. The model predicts that the trajectories that hit the (optimal choice) decision boundary for *A* will tend to have shorter response times than the trajectories that hit the (suboptimal choice) decision boundary *B*. An experimental investigation of this prediction would seem to be impossible without the technique of paying subjects as a function of imperfectly perceived amounts that are perfectly known to the experimenter.

The Distribution of the Noise

Furthermore, McFadden (1974) and Yellott (1977) show that if the error term in a random utility model has a Gumbel (rather than a normal) distribution, then the resulting stochastic choice specification will be the logistic form (Luce, 1959). In other words, the distribution of errors is of great interest to decision researchers. However, conventional designs do not facilitate their study. In contrast, the distribution of errors can be studied with the technique of offering payments for imperfectly perceived and objectively valued stimuli. See Figure 10 for a depiction of the normal probability density and the Gumbel probability density. When compared to the (symmetric) normal distribution, the (asymmetric) Gumbel distribution specifies higher probabilities for large (extreme) events than small events.[56]

These are examples of models that can be difficult to test without psychophysics experimental techniques that provide experimenters with objective values to compare with choice based on subjective perception. In the following section, we describe experiments, which employ incentivized psychophysics techniques, in order to test these models.

We note that the models listed in this section should not be considered as an exhaustive list. Rather, we hope that this discussion can prompt the reader to consider questions that can seem out of reach without incentivized psychophysics experimental techniques.

In summary, the psychophysics experimental designs employ objective stimuli and the experimenter observes behavior that is based on the imperfect perception of these objective stimuli. This produces datasets that are well-positioned to test models that are otherwise difficult to test with standard economic experiments.

5 Incentivized Perceptual Decision-making Literature

While psychophysics insights appear in empirical and theoretical economics, psychophysics experimental techniques are relatively rare in incentivized choice experiments. It is our view that this scarcity reduces the ability of experimental economics to test and improve economic theory. In what follows, we review the experimental papers that employ these psychophysics techniques in materially incentivized designs.[57] In other words, the following describes experiments

---

[56] This feature illustrates why the Gumbel distribution is sometimes referred to as the *Type 1 extreme-value distribution*.

[57] Although providing material incentives for choice in experimental economics is a standard design, it is worth questioning its necessity. Evidence suggests that there are not significant differences in hypothetical or paid responses for either time preference elicitations (Brañas-Garza et al., 2023) or risk preference elicitations (Brañas-Garza et al., 2021). We conjecture that material incentives would be important in experiments where subjects are expected to maintain

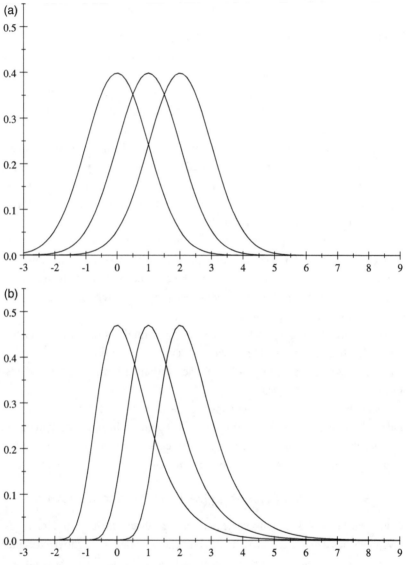

Figure 10 Panel (a) depicts a family of normal densities and Panel (b) depicts a family of Gumbel densities. Every distribution has a variance of 1. The normal distribution is symmetric, whereas the Gumbel distribution has a positive skew, in that the tail on the right is fatter than the tail on the left. This figure is based on figure 1 in Yellott (1977).

---

cognitive effort across many trials. However, only careful experimental observation can address this matter.

where subjects receive monetary payoffs according to their choices in the experiment.

We do not consider every paper where it seems that subjective perception matters for behavior. But rather we restrict attention to papers where the experimenters deliberately manipulate aspects of the design in order to learn about the effects of imperfect perception.

Consider the literature on real effort tasks, where experimenters present subjects with tasks that require effort and subjects are paid based on outcomes related to this effort. The range of techniques in this literature includes incentivizing accurately moving bars (Gill and Prowse, 2012), the number of mazes completed (Gneezy, Niederle, and Rustichini, 2003), the number of items counted (Ariely, Kamenica, and Prelec, 2008; Cabrales, Hernández, and Sánchez, 2020; De Amicis et al, 2020), and tasks requiring both finding and summing (Schram, Brandts, and Gërxhani, 2019).[58]

We admit that effort on many real effort tasks will be affected by the subjects' perception of physical attributes of the interface. However, we do not include these efforts in our discussion because the authors do not manipulate the physical aspects of the interface in an effort to affect the imperfect perception of subjects. In the following, we confine our attention to papers that strive to learn the effects of the imperfect perception.[59] See Table 2 for a summary of the literature that we discuss.

Using Stimuli with Countable Measures to Test Models of Rational Inattention

Some papers, which describe experiments that manipulate the subjective perception of subjects, are designed to test models of rational inattention. For example, Caplin and Dean (2015), Dewan and Neligh (2020), and Dean and Neligh (2023) present subjects with sets of static dots, which can be counted. Caplin et al. (2020) present subjects with sets of different geometric shapes, which can also be counted.[60] These experiments are incentivized in that expected payoffs are increasing in the accuracy on these judgment

---

[58] See Carpenter and Huet-Vaughn (2019) for a recent overview of this literature.

[59] While we do not discuss this literature in further detail, we mention it to acknowledge the role of imperfect perception in experimental economics even when it is not deliberately manipulated and, additionally, we can imagine real effort tasks that are designed to manipulate the imperfect perception.

[60] In a somewhat related test of rational inattention, Khaw, Stevens, and Woodford (2017) present subjects with a sequence of different colored rings and the subjects are tasked to estimate the frequency of the colors. The rings are drawn from a particular distribution, but (undisclosed to the subjects) the distribution is subject to change. The authors find that subjects inattentively respond to changes in the distribution.

Table 2 A summary of the references discussed

Reference	Stimulus type	Designed to be countable	Model tested
Caplin and Dean (2015)	Colored dots	Yes	RI
Dean and Neligh (2023)	Colored dots	Yes	RI
Dewan and Neligh (2020)	Colored dots	Yes	RI
Caplin et al. (2020)	Different polygons	Yes	RI
Duffy et al. (2021)	Length of lines	No	RUM and DDM
Duffy and Smith (2023)	Length of lines	No	RUM and DDM
Bhui (2019a, 2019b)	Dominant direction of moving dots	No	DDM
Pirrone et al. (2018)	Dots of various sizes	Instructed to not	DDM
Zeigenfuse et al. (2014)	Dynamic dots	No	DDM
Pleskac et al. (2019)	Dynamic dots	No	DDM
Dutilh and Rieskamp (2016)	Static dots	Instructed to not	DDM
Heng et al. (2020)	Static dots	No	DDM
Tsetsos et al. (2016)	Heights of dynamic bars	No	DDM
Shevlin et al. (2022)	Arrays of colors	No	DDM
Oud et al. (2016)	Flickering dots	No	DDM
Corgnet et al. (2020)	Color shade	No	Asset market realism
Payzan-LeNestour and Woodford (2022)	Color shade	No	Asset market realism
Goryunov and Rigos (2022)	Location of a dot	No	Game theory realism
Alós-Ferrer and Garagnani (2022b)	Magnitude of integers	No	Realism and DDM

Table 2 (cont.)

Reference	Stimulus type	Designed to be countable	Model tested
Frydman and Jin (2022)	Magnitude of integers	No	Numbers imperfectly perceived
Serences and Saproo (2010)	Orientation of gratings	No	Neuro measures
Weil et al. (2010)	Orientation of gratings	No	Neuro measures
Tavares et al. (2017)	Orientation of lines	No	DDM

Note: RI refers to models of rational inattention; DDM refers to drift diffusion models; RUM refers to random utility models.

tasks. The subjects might have noisy, instantaneous perceptions of the numerosity of the stimuli. However, these experiments are designed to allow the subject to improve their noisy perception by devoting attention to count the objects.

Counting is a costly action, which takes time and cognitive effort. Because the authors know the optimal choice – which is only imperfectly perceived by subjects – the experimenters can use the noise to provide clues about the deliberation. Specifically, the authors use the probability of a correct judgment as a dependent variable in the estimation of latent costs of attention that can inform rational inattention models.

Caplin et al. (2020) present subjects with 24 polygons and give subjects a binary choice regarding which of two polygons is more common. The authors manipulate the material incentives for a correct response (including unincentivized trials) and the difficulty of the choice. See Figure 11 for a screenshot of the task.

The authors find a positive relationship between incentives and performance. Caplin et al. interpret this as the subjects correctly allocating more attention to more incentivized choices, which is consistent with the prediction of rational inattention models. The authors also report that the correct responses are decreasing in the difficulty of the choice, consistent with higher costs of attention.[61]

Dewan and Neligh (2020) direct subjects to indicate the number of static dots. The authors vary the material incentives on the choices. See Figure 12 for a screenshot of this task.

---

[61] It is interesting to note that the authors report a positive relationship between accuracy and response time, which is the opposite of the relationship predicted by Fudenberg, Strack, and Strzalecki (2018). It is possible that numerosity stimuli are different from most other stimuli in this regard.

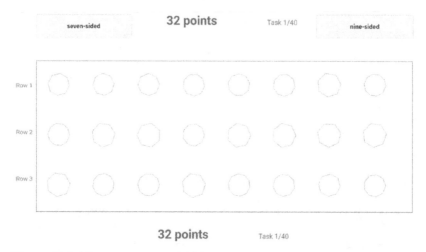

Figure 11 Subjects are presented with regular polygons with seven, eight, nine, and ten sides. Subjects are tasked with determining whether there are more seven-sided polygons or nine-sided polygons. This image is from figure V in Caplin et al. (2020).

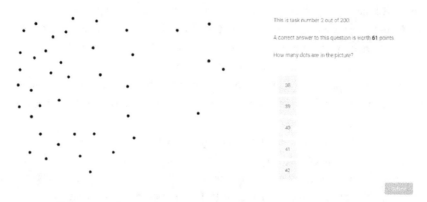

Figure 12 Subjects are presented with a number of dots and are tasked to indicate this number. This image is from figure 8 in Dewan and Neligh (2020).

Dewan and Neligh (2020) note that approximately half of the subjects are not responsive to incentives or consistent with any specification of rational inattention. However, within the set of rationally inattentive subjects who were responsive to incentives, there were four different specifications of the cost-of-attention functions that were best fitting for their choices. Notably, there is evidence that some subjects can be described by continuous cost functions and other subjects can be described by discontinuous cost functions.

Dean and Neligh (2023) describe several experiments where subjects are presented with 100 dots, which are either red or blue. Subjects are tasked with responding to items related to the color composition of the set. The authors find that subjects' responses to incentives are largely consistent with general models of rational inattention. Furthermore, Dean and Neligh report violations of monotonicity, whereby an element b is selected from set $\{a,b,c\}$ more frequently than from set $\{a,b\}$. Note that violations of monotonicity are consistent with rational inattention models but not standard random utility models.

Using Stimuli with Continuous Measures to Study Stochastic Choice

Other studies employ stimuli designed to not be countable by subjects. Duffy and Smith (2023) and Duffy, Gussman, and Smith (2021) describe experiments where subjects are presented with a choice set of lines of various lengths and are paid an amount that is increasing in the length of the selected line. The subjects can only view one line at a time. This implies that the experimenters can observe which lines were viewed. This Mouselab-type[62] design generates process data, where the view clicks provide evidence on the information acquisition of the subject. See Figure 13 for a screenshot of this task.

The authors find evidence of stochastic choice, with the probability of an optimal choice decreasing in the number of lines in the choice set, the similarity of the lengths in the set, and the lengths of the lines in the set.[63]

The nonchoice data also suggests that deliberation is affected by the details of the choice. Subjects view more lines in the trial and have larger response times for choice sets with a larger number of lines, the more similar the lengths in the set, the longer the lengths in the set. Furthermore, the view clicks data suggests that consideration set effects are not primarily driving the stochastic choice because the vast majority of suboptimal choices occur in trials where the longest line was viewed.

Duffy and Smith (2023) and Duffy, Gussman, and Smith (2021) also find that the assumption that errors have a Gumbel distribution fits their data better than the assumption that errors have a normal distribution. This result would seem to support the logistic form of the stochastic choice model of Luce (1959).

The authors also find support for the prediction of Fudenberg, Strack, and Strzalecki (2018): optimal choices tend to have faster response times than suboptimal choices, even when controlling for the heterogeneity of the subjects, the heterogeneity of the choice problems, and the possible endogeneity.

---

[62] See Payne, Bettman, and Johnson (1993).   [63] This is perhaps consistent with Weber's law.

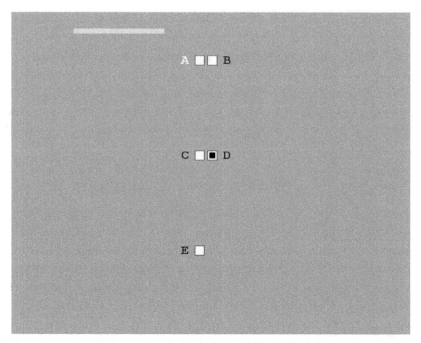

Figure 13 Subjects view the lines by clicking on the corresponding letter label and they indicate their selection by ticking the box adjacent to the label. Subjects can only view one line at a time and they can change their selection before ending the trial. Subjects are paid amounts that are increasing in the length of their selected line. This image is from Duffy and Smith (2023).

Finally, the authors report effects consistent with memory decay and attention. For example, the time between the end of the trial and when the longest line was last viewed is negatively related to the probability of selecting the longest line. Also, the time viewing the longest line is positively related to the probability of selecting the longest line. However, the authors cannot rule out that these memory decay and attention effects are endogenous.

Using Stimuli with Countable Measures to Test Drift Diffusion Models

Other studies employ stimuli that are (in principle) countable, but subjects are not able to count because of time constraints. Bhui (2019a, 2019b) describes experiments where subjects are paid as a function of the accuracy of judging the dominant direction of moving dots. By examining the accuracy with the response times, Bhui is able to scrutinize specifications of DDMs, where agents decide on how much time to devote to a decision. Bhui (2019a) finds that subjects in an online experiment are not sufficiently sensitive to the difficulty manipulations and the incentives. However, Bhui (2019b) finds evidence that laboratory subjects are consistent with the predictions of Fudenberg, Strack, and Strzalecki (2018), including that accurate judgments are associated with shorter response times.

Oud et al. (2016) describe an experiment where subjects are shown two sets of flickering dots and told to select the set with more dots. More difficult decisions, where the sets of dots are more similar, are associated with longer decision times. The authors find that a time limit intervention can improve the probability of an optimal response. Although Duffy and Smith (2023) and Bhui (2019b) report a correlational relationship between optimal choice and response time, it is possible to interpret Oud et al. (2016) as demonstrating a causal relationship.[64]

Using Stimuli with Uncountable Measures to Test Drift Diffusion Models

Tsetsos et al. (2016) describe experiments where subjects are charged with judging the relative heights of bars of dynamic size. Subjects are shown a pair of bars where the height varies within the trial and they are told to select the option with the largest average. Subjects are paid as a function of their accuracy. The authors find that choices violate weak stochastic transitivity, in that A is selected from $\{A,B\}$ with probability greater than 0.5, B is selected from $\{B,C\}$ with probability greater than 0.5, and C is selected from $\{A,B\}$ with probability greater than 0.5. The authors argue that their evidence is consistent with a DDM model of evidence accumulation where large temporary differences are underweighted in the final choice.

Shevlin et al. (2022) incentivize binary judgments of arrays, which contain six color elements. These color elements are drawn from twelve possible colors where each color is assigned a particular value. Therefore, the judgment of which array is more valuable requires the perception of the colors and the addition of the values within the array. The authors fix the material differences between the binary choices and find that higher value array pairs are more accurately judged than lower value array pairs. They also report evidence that higher value array pairs have shorter response times than lower value array pairs. The authors investigate the extent to which their data are consistent with a DDM and find a relationship between the value of the array and the estimated drift rate.

---

[64] Other authors also examine incentivized choices and response times to distinguish among specifications of DDM models using the relative quantity of dynamic dots (Zeigenfuse, Pleskac, and Liu, 2014; Pleskac et al., 2019), the relative quantity of static dots (Dutilh and Rieskamp, 2016; Heng, Woodford, and Polania, 2020), and the quantity of dots of various sizes (Pirrone, Wen, and Li, 2018).

Using Imperfectly Perceived Stimuli to Improve the Realism of the Experiment

Other studies use designs where subjects have an imperfect perception of objective aspects of the setting, in an effort to add realism to the experiment. Corgnet, Hernán-González, and Kujal (2020) describe an experimental asset market where valuations are based on draws from an urn with green and blue chips. In one treatment, the distribution is explicitly given, and in the other treatment, the distribution is represented by the relative faction of the two colors blended together. In this way, the distribution of the urn in the second treatment is imperfectly perceived.[65] The authors find that asset prices are lower in the second treatment and that prices tend to not crash in these markets. Because valuations in real financial markets tend to also be subjectively perceived, this design can be seen as striving to improve the realism of experimental asset markets.

Payzan-LeNestour and Woodford (2022) present a model of outlier blindness, whereby financial investors are not sufficiently attentive to extreme outcomes. Because the value of a financial asset is likely imperfectly perceived, the authors employ stimuli that are imperfectly perceived. Specifically, the authors design an experiment that employs stimuli of twelve different shades of gray that can be ranked by darkness. Subjects make incentivized judgments of darkness for adjacently ranked shades under time pressure. See Figure 14 for a screenshot of this task.

The authors find that adjacent shades are less accurately identified as darker when the recently seen shades are different rather than when the recently seen shades are similar. The authors interpret this result as supporting their model of outlier blindness.

In adding the realism of subjective perception to a strategic setting, Goryunov and Rigos (2022) describe an experiment where subjects play a coordination game with a cutoff strategy based on a payoff-relevant state of the world. However, the state space is conveyed to the subjects based on the location of dot inside a rectangle. In a treatment where subjects are unable to distinguish between small differences in the state, the relationship between actions and the state is smooth and gradual, not unlike that depicted in a psychometric function. In a treatment where subjects are able to distinguish between small differences in the state, actions demonstrate a discrete jump at the theoretical cutoff. This design can be seen investigating the impact of the realism of subjectively perceived states into experimental game theory.

---

[65] The imperfect perception of the distribution of outcomes has also been investigated by using scrambled and unscrambled arrays of colors representing outcomes (Cooper and Rege, 2011) and the use of bingo blower machines that randomly circulate the balls of various colors (Hey, Lotito, and Maffioletti, 2010).

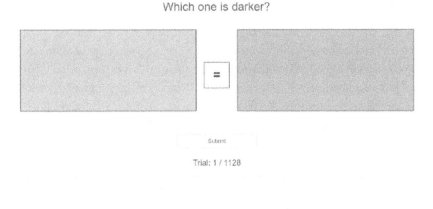

Figure 14 Subjects are tasked to indicate which of the rectangles is darker or if they are equally dark. Subjects are given 2 seconds to make their decision and the remaining time was communicated to the subjects with the bar located below the trial numbers. This image is from figure 3 in Payzan-LeNestour and Woodford (2022).

Alós-Ferrer and Garagnani (2022b) describe an experiment where subjects play a computerized card game with a binary choice. The game has an objectively optimal response, regardless of the subject's attitude toward risk: the optimal choice is based on the relative magnitude of two single-digit integers. However, arriving at the optimal choice requires cognitive effort and the suboptimal choice is selected on a nontrivial number of trials. The authors find that the probability of selecting the optimal choice is increasing in the difference in the expected values of the options. Alós-Ferrer and Garagnani also find that response times are increasing in the difference in the expected values of the options. It seems as if these are consistent with the analogous psychophysics effects appearing in economics decisions. The authors further argue that the response times provide evidence in support of the deliberation processes described by DDMs.

Furthermore, Frydman and Jin (2022) direct subjects to determine whether randomly drawn integers are greater than or less than 65. The experimental payoffs are increasing in the average accuracy of the judgments and decreasing in the average response times. Frydman and Jin find that both errors and response times are increasing when the comparator is closer to 65. The authors also find that the distribution of numbers affects the judgments and the response times. Frydman and Jin interpret this as supporting their model of imperfectly perceived numbers.

Other Incentivized Experiments Employing Imperfectly Perceived Stimuli

Finally, some authors incentivize judgments of imperfectly perceived stimuli that are somewhat difficult to imagine as inducing values in an economics experiment. For example, Serences and Saproo (2010) and Weil et al. (2010) incentivize judgments of the orientation of striped disks (or gratings) while taking measurements of the brain. Finally, Tavares, Perona, and Rangel (2017) incentivize the orientation of lines in order to test a DDM.

Overview of the Reviewed Literature

Earlier, we described several experiments that employ objectively measurable stimuli, which are imperfectly perceived by subjects, and subjects are paid on the basis of their choices. We have also briefly highlighted some of the insights gleaned from employing this experimental technique. It is our hope that our discussion will lead to many new references that study incentivized choice involving imperfectly perceived, but objectively measurable, stimuli.

6 Possible Directions for Experimental Economics

The previous section contained examples of incentivized experiments that employ the technique of presenting subjects with objectively measurable stimuli that are subjectively perceived. In this section, we suggest some possible areas for future research and we conclude with candid advice on reading the brain sciences literature.

More Economics Experiments on Rational Inattention

When reviewing the experimental literature, Dean and Neligh (2023) write, "Overall, there is surprisingly little experimental work in economics testing models of inattention." Furthermore, Maćkowiak, Matějka, and Wiederholt (2023) note that there is much work to be done to improve our understanding of the relationships among the state of the world, attention, beliefs, and actions. Experiments designed with imperfectly perceived stimuli would seem to be well-equipped for this task. We hope that the concepts discussed here are useful in designing experiments that shed light on models of rational inattention.

Multi-attribute Designs

Choice objects can often have multiple attributes, and the methods described in the previous section can be used to understand multi-attribute choice. One interpretation of the dynamic bars design in Tsetsos et al. (2016) is that the subjects are engaged in a multi-attribute choice with each momentary pair of bar heights indicating the measures of one of several equally weighted attributes.

However, there are other available multi-attribute designs where subjects are not passive recipients of sequential stimuli. For example, subjects could be presented with stimuli simultaneously showing multiple dimensions, say both length and width.[66] In this design, subjects could be paid as a function of the area of the selected object or the payment scheme could pay different rates for length and width.

In order to elicit values in more than two attributes, a design could be adapted from Gabaix et al. (2006). Each choice option would have multiple attributes, which combine to constitute its value and only one attribute for an option could be viewed at a time. However, in this design, attribute values are represented by physical stimuli rather than numbers.

Designs Striving for Realism

The values from decisions in realistic settings are rarely known. Often, these values are only imperfectly perceived by the decision-maker. Therefore, the use of such stimuli might strive to improve the realism in economics experiments.

Recall that Corgnet, Hernán-González, and Kujal (2020) induce subjectively perceived values in an experimental asset market by the use of color shade, and this was found to reduce the occurrence of crashes. However, only a single imperfectly perceived stimulus was employed. It is worthwhile exploring behavior in experimental asset markets when different values are induced by imperfectly perceived stimuli.

Likewise, Goryunov and Rigos (2022) induce an imperfectly perceived state of the world in a coordination game but manipulated whether the strategic cutoff was clearly visible. The authors found that in the treatment where the cutoff was not apparent, there was a reduction in the discrete jump at the cutoff.

These experiments serve as examples where the designers strove for realism in the setting and found their results to be less extreme. However, there remain many experimental economics environments where inducing imperfectly perceived values might improve the realism of the experiment and the external validity of the results. We encourage experimenters to think about the settings in which imposing valuations or state variables with numbers brings an undesirable artificiality to the experiment, which could be remedied with the use of an imperfectly perceived stimulus.

---

[66] See Tversky and Russo (1969) for a classic design.

Values Elicited, Not Induced

Our discussion so far has been confined to inducing values with imperfectly perceived stimuli. However, we can also imagine designs where values are elicited with imperfectly perceived stimuli. For example, when a subject is asked for their willingness to pay, another means of eliciting a response is to direct them to indicate a point on an interval that would correspond to the magnitude in their head. Or the subjects could be given a line of adjustable length and asked to respond with the length that best matches the magnitude in their head. This method of eliciting values also has the advantage that there will not be an attraction to round numbers; therefore, the distribution of responses is likely to be smoother than if elicited with numbers.[67]

Eliciting monetary valuations is not the only purpose of providing subjects with a response stimulus that is imperfectly perceived. For instance, subjects might indicate their actions in continuous strategy games by manipulating a magnitude. This could be accomplished by eliciting an action based on the length of an adjustable line or by indicating a point on an interval. Furthermore, beliefs could also be elicited by allowing subjects to vary the fraction of an area filled-in or to indicate a position on an interval.

Another advantage to eliciting subject responses with imperfectly perceived stimuli is that the item could be repeated and the subject's previous response will not be recalled with absolute precision. In this sense, multiple elicitations could be made without giving the subject the opportunity to condition on the previous response: either repeating the response in an effort to be consistent (Falk and Zimmermann, 2013) or offer a deliberately random response (Agranov and Ortoleva, 2017).[68] Furthermore, if subjects have an imprecise memory of their own responses, then feedback-free learning (Weber, 2003) is likely to be diminished.

Reducing the Influence of Cognitive Ability

Both inducing values and eliciting responses with imperfectly perceived stimuli can avoid the need to expose the subjects to numbers. In addition to the advantages mentioned earlier, it is possible that this might reduce the influence

---

[67] There is also evidence that elicitation methods might generate differences in deliberation and responses. Rivera-Garrido et al. (2022) conduct a between-subject experiment where subjective opinions are elicited with a binary (yes/no) scale or a physical slider task, where only the endpoints (0 and 10) are labeled. The authors find that subjects have longer response times and fewer "yes" responses in the slider task.

[68] To observe the difficulty of repeating a question – when both question and answer can be recalled by the subject – consider the following experiment. First, elicit a subject's favorite ice cream flavor. Then, repeat the elicitation several times. Because both the questions and answers are easily recalled, repeated elicitations are unlikely to produce more accurate responses. However, this procedure is likely to result in an exasperated subject.

of cognitive ability. For example, the ability to convert imposed valuations (in the form of numbers) to a magnitude in the subject's head might vary according to cognitive ability. Furthermore, the ability to convert a magnitude in the subject's head into a number (whether valuation, a numeric belief, or a continuous action strategy in a game) might also vary according to cognitive ability.

To the extent that these relationships hold, imposing and eliciting values with imperfectly perceived objects might reduce the effect of cognitive ability on behavior. Specifically in games with a dominant strategy,[69] perhaps representing the payoffs as imperfectly perceived stimuli could mitigate the relationship between responses and cognitive ability.[70] We conjecture that reducing these individual differences based on cognitive ability could aid the analysis of games, for example, improving estimates of the QRE logit precision parameter.

Social Preferences, Complementarities, Process Data, and Material Incentives

It is also an interesting question about how subjects will judge imperfectly perceived stimuli that represent the payoffs of another subject. A natural environment to begin this study of *social preferences* might be representing dictator or ultimatum game payoffs with imperfectly perceived stimuli. Furthermore, the technique of imposing values with imperfectly perceived stimuli might help better explore *complementarities*, where the utility of $x + y$ might not equal the utility of x plus the utility of y.

Some designs hide information from subjects until the subject actively clicks on the relevant portion of the screen. This design generates *process data*, which provide additional clues on the deliberation of the subject. In this particular design, the experimenter can observe what information was viewed and how long the information was viewed. This design, which presents a low-cost, nonintrusive version of eye-tracking, is often referred to as Mouselab.[71] Such a design could help shed light on the social preferences and complementarities experiments described earlier. Additionally, a Mouselab design can help inform consideration set models and very likely has other presently unforeseen benefits to experimental economists.

---

[69] For example, the centipede game or the beauty contest.

[70] For instance, Brañas-Garza, García-Muñoz, and Hernán-González (2012) find a relationship between cognitive reflection test scores and responses in the beauty contest. Also see Brañas-Garza and Smith (2016).

[71] See Payne, Bettman, and Johnson (1993) for the classic reference and see Willemsen and Johnson (2019) for a recent overview.

Another design to generate process data would be similar to Agranov, Caplin, and Tergiman (2015). Rather than making payments contingent only on a final choice, payoffs are based on the choice from a randomly selected second among the fixed, allotted number of seconds. In this way, subjects will strive to make a fast, initial choice but adjust their choice if further deliberation or information changes the decision-maker's mind. In general, this design would also seem to provide an incentivized measure of priors since subjects will want to select the a priori optimal choice as soon as possible. Note that a *standard* response time is available in this design if the subject can end the trial with the understanding that this would expand the current choice onto the remaining seconds. Finally, as suggested by recent evidence in other domains,[72] perhaps the material incentives do not play a significant role in experiments with imperfectly perceived stimuli.

Candid Advice on Reading the Brain Sciences Literature: Be Skeptical

Earlier, we have described some insights from the psychophysics literature that we hope are helpful to the design of economics experiments. A natural continuation of this interest would be for the economist to read the brain sciences literature on their own. While this is clearly encouraged, some advice is warranted. Our general advice is to be skeptical until you are sufficiently convinced of the author's arguments.

Papers – particularly in natural science journals – can be written in a way that makes detecting inaccuracies difficult: authors will often present only a single statistical specification for a result, important experimental design and statistical analysis details will often be relegated to the appendix or omitted, it is often the case that the authors will not report the number of observations on statistical tests, authors can seem casual about possibly endogenous relationships, etc. These common features of papers should encourage, not diminish, the skepticism of the economist reader. Furthermore, some journals might be surprisingly reluctant to admit and correct inaccurate content in their pages.

The following example demonstrates the need for the economist reader to remain skeptical, until convinced otherwise. Consider Körding and Wolpert (2004) – a prominent paper published by *Nature*. The authors describe an experiment where ten subjects are placed into a stochastic environment and the authors claim that there is evidence of *Bayesian* learning. Despite this proclamation of Bayesian learning, the authors do not describe an analysis of

---

[72] Recent contributions do not find evidence that material incentives affect choice in time preference elicitations or in risk preference elicitations. See Brañas-Garza et al. (2021) and Brañas-Garza et al. (2023).

behavior across trials.[73] Simply based on this, the reader should be skeptical of their claim of learning.

Duffy et al. (2022) reanalyze their data by examining behavior across trials and do not find evidence of learning of any kind, particularly Bayesian learning. Instead, Duffy et al. (2022) find that there is a bias toward recent stimuli, and when averaged across trials, this can incorrectly appear to be consistent with learning. Furthermore, Duffy et al. (2022) find that Körding and Wolpert (2004) mischaracterize key experimental design features.[74]

We mention another matter to consider when reading papers from the brain sciences literature. Authors will often present a *computational model*, which is effectively a computer simulation that generates a distribution of behavior. These models are often opaque, in that it is difficult for the reader to reproduce or independently verify the results. Furthermore, the proposed computational model is often run in competition with a set of other computational models. Clearly a model's proponent has an incentive to pick lackluster competitors.

One clear advantage of these computational models is that they can generate a joint distribution between two (possibly) endogenous variables. For example, a computational model could be used to generate joint predictions on response times and the decision quality. Specifically, the computational model might make a prediction that all things equal (fixing the heterogeneity of the subjects and the heterogeneity of the choice problems) that longer response times will tend to be associated with worse decisions. This would be an interesting prediction.

However, a computational model cannot determine whether a particular set of experimental observations behave in this manner. Only careful econometric analysis could support this claim. Otherwise, it remains possible that the result is driven by unobserved subject-level heterogeneity (slower subjects also make worse decisions) or unobserved choice-level heterogeneity (more difficult choices tend to be slower and have worse decisions). In this sense, researchers will sometimes regard a computational model as a substitute for careful econometric analysis, particularly when there is possible endogeneity. The economist reader should be skeptical when it seems as if authors regard computational models as substitutes for careful econometric analysis.

---

[73] This omission becomes even more surprising, given the great efforts to characterize learning across trials in the classic psychology literature. See Bush and Mosteller (1955) for a classic overview.

[74] These matters in Körding and Wolpert (2004) remain unaddressed in the pages of *Nature*.

Final Thoughts

We hope that experimental economists keep the following in mind. Subjects have an imperfect perception of objectively measurable stimuli. These imperfect perceptions generate stochastic choice. However, because the experimenter knows the objective measures of the stimuli, the stochastic choice gives clues that are not available if the objective measure is not known to the experimenter. The use of nonchoice data can provide clues about the deliberation process. With these insights, we hope that experimental economics will strive to uncover what is hiding in the noise. Although we have described some specific domains where psychophysics experimental techniques have been employed, we are confident that there remain many previously unconsidered applications that will help uncover hidden insights of interest to economists.

References

Acharya, Sushant, and Wee, Shu Lin (2020): "Rational inattention in hiring decisions," *American Economic Journal: Macroeconomics*, 12(1), 1–40.

Agranov, Marina, Caplin, Andrew, and Tergiman, Chloe (2015): "Naive play and the process of choice in guessing games," *Journal of the Economic Science Association*, 1(2), 146–157.

Agranov, Marina, and Ortoleva, Pietro (2017): "Stochastic choice and preferences for randomization," *Journal of Political Economy*, 125(1), 40–68.

Allred, Sarah R., Crawford, L. Elizabeth, Duffy, Sean, and Smith, John (2016): "Working memory and spatial judgments: Cognitive load increases the central tendency bias," *Psychonomic Bulletin and Review*, 23(6), 1825–1831.

Alós-Ferrer, Carlos, Fehr, Ernst, and Netzer, Nick (2021): "Time will tell: Recovering preferences when choices are noisy," *Journal of Political Economy*, 129(6), 1828–1877.

Alós-Ferrer, Carlos, and Garagnani, Michele (2021): "Choice consistency and strength of preference," *Economics Letters*, 198, 109672.

Alós-Ferrer, Carlos, and Garagnani, Michele (2022a): "Strength of preference and decisions under risk," *Journal of Risk and Uncertainty*, 64, 309–329.

Alós-Ferrer, Carlos, and Garagnani, Michele (2022b): "The gradual nature of economic errors," *Journal of Economic Behavior and Organization*, 200, 55–66.

Amador-Hidalgo, Luis, Brañas-Garza, Pablo, Espín, Antonio M., García-Muñoz, Teresa, and Hernández-Román, Ana (2021): "Cognitive abilities and risk-taking: Errors, not preferences," *European Economic Review*, 134, 103694.

American Psychological Association (2010): *Publication Manual of the American Psychological Association*. Washington, DC, 6th ed.

Anderson, Norman H. (1970): "Functional measurement and psychophysical judgment," *Psychological Review*, 77(3), 153–170.

Antonides, Gerrit (2008): "How is perceived inflation related to actual price changes in the European Union?" *Journal of Economic Psychology*, 29(4), 417–432.

Antonides, Gerrit, Verhoef, Peter C., and Van Aalst, Marcel (2002): "Consumer perception and evaluation of waiting time: A field experiment," *Journal of Consumer Psychology*, 12(3), 193–202.

Apesteguia, Jose, and Ballester, Miguel A. (2021): "Separating predicted randomness from residual behavior," *Journal of the European Economic Association*, 19(2), 1041–1076.

Apesteguia, Jose, Ballester, Miguel A., and Lu, Jay (2017): "Single-crossing random utility models," *Econometrica*, 85(2), 661–674.

Argenziano, Rossella, and Gilboa, Itzhak (2017): "Psychophysical foundations of the Cobb–Douglas utility function," *Economics Letters*, 157, 21–23.

Ariely, Dan, Kamenica, Emir, and Prelec, Dražen (2008): "Man's search for meaning: The case of Legos," *Journal of Economic Behavior and Organization*, 67(3–4), 671–677.

Ballinger, T. Parker, and Wilcox, Nathaniel T. (1997): "Decisions, error and heterogeneity," *Economic Journal*, 107(443), 1090–1105.

Bayrak, Oben K., and Hey, John D. (2020): "Understanding preference imprecision," *Journal of Economic Surveys*, 34(1), 154–174.

Bazerman, Max H., and Samuelson, William F. (1983): "I won the auction but don't want the prize," *Journal of Conflict Resolution*, 27(4), 618–634.

Becker, Gordon M., DeGroot, Morris H., and Marschak, Jacob (1963): "Stochastic models of choice behavior," *Systems Research and Behavioral Science*, 8(1), 41–55.

Bernasconi, Michele, and Seri, Raffaello (2016): "What are we estimating when we fit Stevens' power law?" *Journal of Mathematical Psychology*, 75, 137–149.

Bernoulli, Daniel (1738): "Exposition of a new theory on the measurement of risk," (translated by Sommer, Louise (1954): *Econometrica*, 22(1), 23–36).

Bhui, Rahul (2019a): "A statistical test for the optimality of deliberative time allocation," *Psychonomic Bulletin and Review*, 26(3), 855–867.

Bhui, Rahul (2019b): "Testing optimal timing in value-linked decision making," *Computational Brain and Behavior*, 2(2), 85–94.

Blavatskyy, Pavlo R. (2008): "Stochastic utility theorem," *Journal of Mathematical Economics*, 44, 1049–1056.

Blavatskyy, Pavlo R. (2011): "Probabilistic risk aversion with an arbitrary outcome set," *Economics Letters*, 112(1), 34–37.

Boldrin, Michele, Christiano, Lawrence J., and Fisher, Jonas D. M. (2001): "Habit persistence, asset returns, and the business cycle," *American Economic Review*, 91(1), 149–166.

Bordalo, Pedro, Gennaioli, Nicola, and Shleifer, Andrei (2012): "Salience theory of choice under risk," *Quarterly Journal of Economics*, 127(3), 1243–1285.

Brañas-Garza, Pablo, Ductor, Lorenzo, and Kovářík, Jaromír (2022): "The role of unobservable characteristics in friendship network formation," Working paper, ArXiv:2206.13641.

Brañas-Garza, Pablo, Estepa-Mohedano, Lorenzo, Jorrat, Diego, Orozco, Victor, and Rascon-Ramirez, Ericka (2021): "To pay or not to pay: Measuring risk preferences in lab and field," *Judgment and Decision Making*, 16 (5), 1290–1313.

Brañas-Garza, Pablo, García-Muñoz, Teresa, and Hernán-González, Roberto (2012): "Cognitive effort in the beauty contest game," *Journal of Economic Behavior and Organization*, 83(2), 254–260.

Brañas-Garza, Pablo, Jorrat, Diego, Espín, Antonio M., and Sánchez, Angel (2023): "Paid and hypothetical time preferences are the same: Lab, field and online evidence," *Experimental Economics*, 26, 412–434.

Brañas-Garza, Pablo, and Smith, John (2016): "Cognitive abilities and economic behavior," *Journal of Behavioral and Experimental Economics*, 64, 1–4.

Brocas, Isabelle, Carrillo, Juan D., and Tarrasó, Jorge (2018): "How long is a minute?" *Games and Economic Behavior*, 111, 305–322.

Bruni, Luigino, and Sugden, Robert (2007): "The road not taken: How psychology was removed from economics, and how it might be brought back," *Economic Journal*, 117(516), 146–173.

Bush, Robert R., and Mosteller, Frederick (1955): *Stochastic Models for Learning*. John Wiley, New York.

Butler, David J. (2000): "Do non-expected utility choice patterns spring from hazy preferences? An experimental study of choice errors," *Journal of Economic Behavior and Organization*, 41(3), 277–297.

Butler, David J., and Loomes, Graham C. (2007): "Imprecision as an account of the preference reversal phenomenon," *American Economic Review*, 97(1), 277–297.

Cabrales, Antonio, Hernández, Penélope, and Sánchez, Angel (2020): "Robots, labor markets, and universal basic income," *Humanities and Social Sciences Communications*, 7, 185.

Camerer, Colin F., and Ho, Teck-Hua (1994): "Violations of the betweenness axiom and nonlinearity in probability," *Journal of Risk and Uncertainty*, 8(2), 167–196.

Capen, Edward C., Clapp, Robert V., and Campbell, William M. (1971): "Competitive bidding in high-risk situations," *Journal of Petroleum Technology*, 23(6), 641–653.

Caplin, Andrew (2012): "Choice sets as percepts," in *Neuroscience of Preference and Choice: Cognitive and Neural Mechanisms*, Dolan, Raymond, and Sharot, Tali (Eds.), Academic Press, Waltham, 295–304.

Caplin, Andrew, Csaba, Dániel, Leahy, John, and Nov, Oded (2020): "Rational inattention, competitive supply, and psychometrics," *Quarterly Journal of Economics*, 135(3), 1681–1724.

Caplin, Andrew, and Dean, Mark (2015): "Revealed preference, rational inattention, and costly information acquisition," *American Economic Review*, 105(7), 2183–2203.

Carpenter, Jeffrey, and Huet-Vaughn, Emiliano (2019): "Real-effort tasks," in *Handbook of Research Methods and Applications in Experimental Economics*, Schram, Arthur, and Ule, Aljaž (Eds.), Edward Elgar, Cheltenham, 368–383.

Case, Karl E., Quigley, John M., and Shiller, Robert J. (2005): "Comparing wealth effects: The stock market versus the housing market," *Advances in Macroeconomics*, 5(1), Article 1.

Cerreia-Vioglio, Simone, Dillenberger, David, Ortoleva, Pietro, and Riella, Gil (2019): "Deliberately stochastic," *American Economic Review*, 109(7), 2425–2445.

Churcher, B. G. (1935): "A loudness scale for industrial noise measurements," *Journal of the Acoustical Society of America*, 6(4), 216–225.

Cooper, David J., and Rege, Mari (2011): "Misery loves company: Social regret and social interaction effects in choices under risk and uncertainty," *Games and Economic Behavior*, 73(1), 91–110.

Corgnet, Brice, Hernán-González, Roberto, and Kujal, Praveen (2020): "On booms that never bust: Ambiguity in experimental asset markets with bubbles," *Journal of Economic Dynamics and Control*, 110, 103754.

De Amicis, Luisa, Binenti, Silvia, Maciel Cardoso et al. (2020): "Understanding drivers when investing for impact: An experimental study," *Palgrave Communications*, 6, 86.

Dean, Mark, and Neligh, Nathaniel (2023): "Experimental tests of rational inattention," *Journal of Political Economy*, forthcoming.

Debreu, Gerard (1960): "Individual choice behavior: A theoretical analysis," *American Economic Review*, 50(1), 186–188.

Dessein, Wouter, Galeotti, Andrea, and Santos, Tano (2016): "Rational inattention and organizational focus," *American Economic Review*, 106(6), 1522–1536.

Dewan, Ambuj, and Neligh, Nathaniel (2020): "Estimating information cost functions in models of rational inattention," *Journal of Economic Theory*, 187, 105011.

Duffy, Sean, Gussman, Steven, and Smith, John (2021): "Visual judgments of length in the economics laboratory: Are there brains in stochastic choice?" *Journal of Behavioral and Experimental Economics*, 93, 101708.

Duffy, Sean, Hertel, Johanna, Igan, Deniz, Pinheiro, Marcelo, and Smith, John (2022): "On Bayesian integration in sensorimotor learning: Another look at Kording and Wolpert (2004)," *Cortex*, 153, 87–96.

Duffy, Sean, and Smith, John (2020): "On the category adjustment model: Another look at Huttenlocher, Hedges, and Vevea (2000)," *Mind and Society*, 19(1), 163–193.

Duffy, Sean, and Smith, John (2023): "An economist and a psychologist form a line: What can imperfect perception of length tell us about stochastic choice?" Working paper, Rutgers University-Camden.

Dutilh, Gilles, and Rieskamp, Jörg (2016): "Comparing perceptual and preferential decision making," *Psychonomic Bulletin and Review*, 23(3), 723–737.

Eliaz, Kfir, and Spiegler, Ran (2011): "Consideration sets and competitive marketing," *Review of Economic Studies*, 78(1), 235–262.

Engen, Trygg, and Tulunay, Ülker (1957): "Some sources of error in half-heaviness judgments," *Journal of Experimental Psychology*, 54(3), 208–212.

Evans, Nathan J., and Wagenmakers, Eric-Jan (2020): "Evidence accumulation models: Current limitations and future directions," *Quantitative Methods for Psychology*, 16(2), 73–90.

Falk, Armin, and Zimmermann, Florian (2013): "A taste for consistency and survey response behavior," *CESifo Economic Studies*, 59(1), 181–193.

Falmagne, Jean-Claude (2002): *Elements of Psychophysical Theory*. Oxford University Press, New York.

Fechner, Gustav Theodor (1860): *Elemente der Psychophysik*. (*Elements of psychophysics*, translated 1966. Holt, Rinehart, and Winston, New York.)

Frydman, Cary, and Jin, Lawrence J. (2022): "Efficient coding and risky choice," *Quarterly Journal of Economics*, 137(1), 161–213.

Fudenberg, Drew, Iijima, Ryota, and Strzalecki, Tomasz (2015): "Stochastic choice and revealed perturbed utility," *Econometrica*, 83(6), 2371–2409.

Fudenberg, Drew, Newey, Whitney, Strack, Philipp, and Strzalecki, Tomasz (2020): "Testing the drift-diffusion model," *Proceedings of the National Academy of Sciences*, 117(52), 33141–33148.

Fudenberg, Drew, Strack, Philipp, and Strzalecki, Tomasz (2018): "Speed, accuracy, and the optimal timing of choices," *American Economic Review*, 108(12), 3651–3684.

Gabaix, Xavier, Laibson, David, Moloche, Guillermo, and Weinberg, Stephen (2006): "Costly information acquisition: Experimental analysis of a boundedly rational model," *American Economic Review*, 96(4), 1043–1068.

Gescheider, George A. (1997): *Psychophysics: The Fundamentals*. Routledge Press, New York.

Gescheider, George A., Wright, John H., and Polak, John W. (1971): "Detection of vibrotactile signals differing in probability of occurrence," *Journal of Psychology*, 78(2), 253–260.

Gill, David, and Prowse, Victoria (2012): "A structural analysis of disappointment aversion in a real effort competition," *American Economic Review*, 102(1), 469–503.

Gneezy, Uri, Niederle, Muriel, and Rustichini, Aldo (2003): "Performance in competitive environments: Gender differences," *Quarterly Journal of Economics*, 118(3), 1049–1074.

Goeree, Jacob K., Holt, Charles A., and Palfrey, Thomas R. (2003): "Risk averse behavior in generalized matching pennies games," *Games and Economic Behavior*, 45(1), 97–113.

Goeree, Jacob K., Holt, Charles A., and Palfrey, Thomas R. (2010): "Quantal response equilibria," in *Behavioural and Experimental Economics*, Durlauf, Steven N., Blume, Lawrence E. (Eds.), New Palgrave Economics Collection, Palgrave Macmillan, New York, 234–242.

Gonzalez, Richard, and Wu, George (1999): "On the shape of the probability weighting function," *Cognitive Psychology*, 38(1), 129–166.

Goryunov, Maxim, and Rigos, Alexandros (2022): "Discontinuous and continuous stochastic choice and coordination in the lab," *Journal of Economic Theory*, 206, 105557.

Hausman, Jerry A., and Wise, David A. (1978): "A conditional probit model for qualitative choice: Discrete decisions recognizing interdependence and heterogeneous preferences," *Econometrica*, 46(2), 403–426.

Hautus, Michael J., Macmillan, Neil A., and Creelman, C. Douglas (2022): *Detection Theory: A User's Guide*. Routledge, New York.

Heinemann, Frank, Nagel, Rosemarie, and Ockenfels, Peter (2009): "Measuring strategic uncertainty in coordination games," *Review of Economic Studies*, 76(1), 181–221.

Heng, Joseph A., Woodford, Michael, and Polania, Rafael (2020): "Efficient sampling and noisy decisions," *eLife*, 9, e54962.

Henmon, V. A. C. (1911): "The relation of the time of a judgment to its accuracy," *Psychological Review*, 18(3), 186–201.

Hey, John D. (1995): "Experimental investigations of errors in decision making under risk," *European Economic Review*, 39(3–4), 633–640.

Hey, John D. (2001): "Does repetition improve consistency?" *Experimental Economics*, 4(1), 5–54.

Hey, John D. (2005): "Why we should not be silent about noise," *Experimental Economics*, 8(4), 325–345.

Hey, John D., Lotito, Gianna, and Maffioletti, Anna (2010): "The descriptive and predictive adequacy of theories of decision making under uncertainty/ ambiguity," *Journal of Risk and Uncertainty*, 41(2), 81–111.

Hey, John D., and Orme, Chris (1994): "Investigating generalizations of expected utility theory using experimental data," *Econometrica*, 62(6), 1291–1326.

Hildenbrand, Werner (1971): "Random preferences and equilibrium analysis," *Journal of Economic Theory*, 3(4), 414–429.

Hollingworth, Harry Levi (1910): "The central tendency of judgment," *Journal of Philosophy, Psychology and Scientific Methods*, 7(17), 461–469.

Horan, Sean, Manzini, Paola, and Mariotti, Marco (2022): "When is coarseness not a curse? Comparative statics of the coarse random utility model," *Journal of Economic Theory*, 202, 105445.

Huber, Joel, Payne, John W., and Puto, Christopher (1982): "Adding asymmetrically dominated alternatives: Violations of regularity and the similarity hypothesis," *Journal of Consumer Research*, 9(1), 90–98.

Huttenlocher, Janellen, Hedges, Larry V., and Vevea, Jack L. (2000): "Why do categories affect stimulus judgment?" *Journal of Experimental Psychology: General*, 129(2), 220–241.

Kahneman, Daniel, and Tversky, Amos (1979): "Prospect theory: An analysis of decision under risk," *Econometrica*, 47(2), 263–292.

Kellogg, W. N. (1931): "The time of judgment in psychometric measures," *American Journal of Psychology*, 43(1), 65–86.

Khaw, Mel Win, Li, Ziang, and Woodford, Michael (2021): "Cognitive imprecision and small-stakes risk aversion," *Review of Economic Studies*, 88(4), 1979–2013.

Khaw, Mel Win, Stevens, Luminita, and Woodford, Michael (2017): "Discrete adjustment to a changing environment: Experimental evidence," *Journal of Monetary Economics*, 91, 88–103.

Kingdom, Frederick A., and Prins, Nicolaas (2016): *Psychophysics: A Practical Introduction*. Elsevier Science and Technology, San Diego .

Körding, Konrad P., and Wolpert, Daniel M. (2004): "Bayesian integration in sensorimotor learning," *Nature*, 427(6971), 244–247.

Krishna, Vijay (2002): *Auction Theory*. Academic Press, San Diego.

Krueger, Lester E. (1989): "Reconciling Fechner and Stevens: Toward a unified psychophysical law," *Behavioral and Brain Sciences*, 12(2), 251–267.

Laming, Donald (1986): *Sensory Analysis*. Academic Press, Orlando.

Lévy-Garboua, Louis, Maafi, Hela, Masclet, David, and Terracol, Antoine (2012): "Risk aversion and framing effects," *Experimental Economics*, 15(1), 128–144.

Liang, Annie (2019): "Inference of preference heterogeneity from choice data," *Journal of Economic Theory*, 179, 275–311.

Loomes, Graham (2005): "Modelling the stochastic component of behaviour in experiments: Some issues for the interpretation of data," *Experimental Economics*, 8(4), 301–323.

Loomes, Graham, Starmer, Chris, and Sugden, Robert (1989): "Preference reversal: Information-processing effect or rational non-transitive choice?" *Economic Journal*, 99(395), 140–151.

Loomis, John, Peterson, George, Champ, Patricia, Brown, Thomas, and Lucero, Beatrice (1998): "Paired comparison estimates of willingness to accept versus contingent valuation estimates of willingness to pay," *Journal of Economic Behavior and Organization*, 35(4), 501–515.

Lu, Jay (2016): "Random choice and private information," *Econometrica*, 84 (6), 1983–2027.

Luce, R. Duncan (1959): *Individual Choice Behavior: A Theoretical Analysis*. Wiley, New York.

Luce, R. Duncan, and Green, David M. (1972): "A neural timing theory for response times and the psychophysics of intensity," *Psychological Review*, 79 (1), 14–57.

Machina, Mark J. (1985): "Stochastic choice functions generated from deterministic preferences over lotteries," *Economic Journal*, 95(379), 575–594.

Maćkowiak, Bartosz, Matějka, Filip, and Wiederholt, Mirko (2023): "Rational inattention: A review," *Journal of Economic Literature*, 61(1), 226–273.

Maćkowiak, Bartosz, and Wiederholt, Mirko (2009): "Optimal sticky prices under rational inattention," *American Economic Review*, 99(3), 769–803.

Maćkowiak, Bartosz, and Wiederholt, Mirko (2015): "Business cycle dynamics under rational inattention," *Review of Economic Studies*, 82(4), 1502–1532.

Manzini, Paola, and Mariotti, Marco (2014): "Stochastic choice and consideration sets," *Econometrica*, 82(3), 1153–1176.

Mas-Colell, Andreu, Whinston, Michael D., and Green, Jerry R. (1995): *Microeconomic Theory*. Oxford University Press, Oxford.

Masatlioglu, Yusufcan, Nakajima, Daisuke, and Ozbay, Erkut Y. (2012): "Revealed attention," *American Economic Review*, 102(5), 2183–2205.

Matějka, Filip, and McKay, Alisdair (2015): "Rational inattention to discrete choices: A new foundation for the multinomial logit model," *American Economic Review*, 105(1), 272–298.

McFadden, Daniel (1974): "Conditional logit analysis of qualitative choice behavior," in *Frontiers in Econometrics*, Zarembka, Paul (Ed.), Academic Press, New York, 105–142.

McFadden, Daniel (2001): "Economic choices," *American Economic Review*, 91(3), 351–378.

McKelvey, Richard D., and Palfrey, Thomas R. (1995): "Quantal response equilibria for normal form games," *Games and Economic Behavior*, 10(1), 6–38.

Mead, Walter J., Moseidjord, Asbjorn, and Sorensen, Philip E. (1983): "The rate of return earned by lessees under cash bonus bidding for OCS oil and gas leases," *Energy Journal*, 4(4), 37–52.

Mondria, Jordi, and Wu, Thomas (2010): "The puzzling evolution of the home bias, information processing and financial openness," *Journal of Economic Dynamics and Control*, 34(5), 875–896.

Mosteller, Frederick, and Nogee, Philip (1951): "An experimental measurement of utility," *Journal of Political Economy*, 59(5), 371–404.

Munsell, Albert E. O., Sloan, Louise L., and Godlove, Isaac H. (1933): "Neutral value scales. I. Munsell neutral value scale," *Journal of the Optical Society of America*, 23(11), 394–411.

Murray, David J. (1993): "A perspective for viewing the history of psychophysics," *Behavioral and Brain Sciences*, 16(1), 115–137.

Naeher, Dominik (2022): "Technology adoption under costly information processing," *International Economic Review*, 63(2), 699–753.

Natenzon, Paulo (2019): "Random choice and learning," *Journal of Political Economy*, 127(1), 419–457.

Navarro-Martinez, Daniel, Loomes, Graham, Isoni, Andrea, Butler, David, and Alaoui, Larbi (2018): "Boundedly rational expected utility theory," *Journal of Risk and Uncertainty*, 57(3), 199–223.

Ochs, Jack (1995): "Games with unique, mixed strategy equilibria: An experimental study," *Games and Economic Behavior*, 10(1), 202–217.

Okunade, Albert A. (1992): "Functional forms and habit effects in the US demand for coffee," *Applied Economics*, 24(11), 1203–1212.

Oud, Bastiaan, Krajbich, Ian, Miller, Kevin et al. (2016): "Irrational time allocation in decision-making," *Proceedings of the Royal Society B: Biological Sciences*, 283(1822), 20151439.

Payne, John W., Bettman, James R., and Johnson, Eric J. (1993): *The Adaptive Decision Maker*, Cambridge University Press, Cambridge.

Payzan-LeNestour, Elise, and Woodford, Michael (2022): "Outlier blindness: A neurobiological foundation for neglect of financial risk," *Journal of Financial Economics*, 143(3), 1316–1343.

Pirrone, Angelo, Wen, Wen, and Li, Sheng (2018): "Single-trial dynamics explain magnitude sensitive decision making," *BMC Neuroscience*, 19, 54.

Plateau, Joseph Antoine Ferdinand (1872): "Sur la mesure des sensations physiques, et sur la loi qui lie l'intensité de la cause excitante," *Bulletins de l'Academie Royale des Sciences, des Lettres, et des Beaux-Arts de Belgique*, 33, 376–388.

Pleskac, Timothy J., Yu, Shuli, Hopwood, Christopher, and Liu, Taosheng (2019): "Mechanisms of deliberation during preferential choice: Perspectives from computational modeling and individual differences," *Decision*, 6(1), 77–107.

Pratt, John W., Wise, David A., and Zeckhauser, Richard (1979): "Price differences in almost competitive markets," *Quarterly Journal of Economics*, 93 (2), 189–211.

Prelec, Drazen (1998): "The probability weighting function," *Econometrica*, 66 (3), 497–527.

Rabin, Matthew (2000): "Risk aversion and expected-utility theory: A calibration theorem," *Econometrica*, 68(5), 1281–1292.

Ratcliff, Roger (1978): "A theory of memory retrieval," *Psychological Review*, 85(2), 59–108.

Ratcliff, Roger (2014): "Measuring psychometric functions with the diffusion model," *Journal of Experimental Psychology: Human Perception and Performance*, 40(2), 870–888.

Ratcliff, Roger, and McKoon, Gail (2008): "The diffusion decision model: Theory and data for two-choice decision tasks," *Neural Computation*, 20(4), 873–922.

Ratcliff, Roger, and Rouder, Jeffrey N. (1998): "Modeling response times for two-choice decisions," *Psychological Science*, 9(5), 347–356.

Reutskaja, Elena, Nagel, Rosemarie, Camerer, Colin F., and Rangel, Antonio (2011): "Search dynamics in consumer choice under time pressure: An eye-tracking study," *American Economic Review*, 101(2), 900–926.

Rivera-Garrido, Noelia, Ramos-Sosa, M. P., Accerenzi, Michela, and Brañas-Garza, Pablo (2022): "Continuous and binary sets of responses are not the same: Evidence from the field," *Scientific Reports*, 12, 14376.

Roberts, John H., and Lattin, James M. (1991): "Development and testing of a model of consideration set composition," *Journal of Marketing Research*, 28(4), 429–440.

Rodríguez, Jorge, Urzúa, Sergio, and Reyes, Loreto (2016): "Heterogeneous economic returns to post-secondary degrees: Evidence from Chile," *Journal of Human Resources*, 51(2), 416–460.

Rozen, Kareen (2010): "Foundations of intrinsic habit formation," *Econometrica*, 78(4), 1341–1373.

Rustichini, Aldo, and Siconolfi, Paolo (2014): "Dynamic theory of preferences: Habit formation and taste for variety," *Journal of Mathematical Economics*, 55, 55–68.

Salomon, Joshua A., and Murray, Christopher J. L. (2004): "A multi-method approach to measuring health-state valuations," *Health Economics*, 13(3), 281–290.

Savage, Leonard J. (1954): *The Foundations of Statistics*. Wiley, New York. Reprinted in 1972 by Dover, New York.

Schram, Arthur, Brandts, Jordi, and Gërxhani, Klarita (2019): "Social-status ranking: A hidden channel to gender inequality under competition," *Experimental Economics*, 22(2), 396–418.

See, Judi E., Warm, Joel S., Dember, William N., and Howe, Steven R. (1997): "Vigilance and signal detection theory: An empirical evaluation of five measures of response bias," *Human Factors*, 39(1), 14–29.

Serences, John T., and Saproo, Sameer (2010): "Population response profiles in early visual cortex are biased in favor of more valuable stimuli," *Journal of Neurophysiology*, 104(1), 76–87.

Shepard, Roger N. (1981): "Psychological relations and psychophysical scales: On the status of 'direct' psychophysical measurement," *Journal of Mathematical Psychology*, 24(1), 21–57.

Shevlin, Blair R. K., Smith, Stephanie M., Hausfeld, Jan, and Krajbich, Ian (2022): "High-value decisions are fast and accurate, inconsistent with diminishing value sensitivity," *Proceedings of the National Academy of Sciences*, 119(6), e2101508119.

Shocker, Allan D., Ben-Akiva, Moshe, Boccara, Bruno, and Nedungadi, Prakash (1991): "Consideration set influences on consumer decision-making and choice: Issues, models, and suggestions," *Marketing Letters*, 2(3), 181–197.

Sims, Christopher A. (2003): "Implications of rational inattention," *Journal of Monetary Economics*, 50(3), 665–690.

Sinn, Hans-Werner (1985): "Psychophysical laws in risk theory," *Journal of Economic Psychology*, 6(2), 185–206.

Smith, Vernon L. (1976): "Experimental economics: Induced value theory," *American Economic Review*, 66(2), 274–279.

Solomon, Joshua A. (2009): "The history of dipper functions," *Attention, Perception, & Psychophysics*, 71(3), 435–443.

Stevens, Luminita (2020): "Coarse pricing policies," *Review of Economic Studies*, 87(1), 420–453.

Stevens, S. S. (1936): "A scale for the measurement of a psychological magnitude: Loudness," *Psychological Review*, 43(5), 405–416.

Stevens, S. S. (1956): "The direct estimation of sensory magnitudes: Loudness," *American Journal of Psychology*, 69(1), 1–25.

Stevens, S. S. (1957): "On the psychophysical law," *Psychological Review*, 64(3), 153–181.

Stevens, S. S. (1960): "The psychophysics of sensory function," *American Scientist*, 48(2), 226–253.

Stevens, S. S. (1961): "To honor Fechner and repeal his law: A power function, not a log function, describes the operating characteristic of a sensory system," *Science*, 133(3446), 80–86.

Stevens, S. S. (1971): "Issues in psychophysical measurement," *Psychological Review*, 78(5), 426–450.

Stevens, S. S., and Guirao, Miguelina (1962): "Loudness, reciprocality, and partition scales," *Journal of the Acoustical Society of America*, 34.9B, 1466–1471.

Stigler, George J. (1950a): "The development of utility theory. I," *Journal of Political Economy*, 58(4), 307–327.

Stigler, George J. (1950b): "The development of utility theory. II," *Journal of Political Economy*, 58(5), 373–396.

Summerfield, Christopher, and Tsetsos, Konstantinos (2012): "Building bridges between perceptual and economic decision-making: Neural and computational mechanisms," *Frontiers in Neuroscience*, 6, 70.

Swets, John A., Tanner Jr, Wilson P., and Birdsall, Theodore G. (1961): "Decision processes in perception," *Psychological Review*, 68(5), 301–340.

Takahashi, Taiki (2011): "Psychophysics of the probability weighting function," *Physica A: Statistical Mechanics and its Applications*, 390(5), 902–905.

Tanner, W. P., Swets, J. A., and Green, D. M. (1956): "Some general properties of the hearing mechanism," University of Michigan, Electronic Defense Group, Technical Report No. 30.

Taubinsky, Dmitry, and Rees-Jones, Alex (2018): "Attention variation and welfare: Theory and evidence from a tax salience experiment," *Review of Economic Studies*, 85(4), 2462–2496.

Tavares, Gabriela, Perona, Pietro, and Rangel, Antonio (2017): "The attentional drift diffusion model of simple perceptual decision-making," *Frontiers in Neuroscience*, 11, 468.

Thaler, Richard (1980): "Toward a positive theory of consumer choice," *Journal of Economic Behavior and Organization*, 1(1), 39–60.

Thaler, Richard (1988): "Anomalies: The winner's curse," *Journal of Economic Perspectives*, 2(1), 191–202.

Thurstone, L. L. (1927a): "A law of comparative judgment," *Psychological Review*, 34(4), 273–286.

Thurstone, L. L. (1927b): "Psychophysical analysis," *American Journal of Psychology*, 38(3), 368–389.

Train, Kenneth E. (2009): *Discrete Choice Methods with Simulation*. Cambridge University Press, Cambridge.

Tserenjigmid, Gerelt (2020): "On the characterization of linear habit formation," *Economic Theory*, 70(1), 49–93.

Tsetsos, Konstantinos, Moran, Rani, Moreland, James et al. (2016): "Economic irrationality is optimal during noisy decision making," *Proceedings of the National Academy of Sciences*, 113(11), 3102–3107.

Tversky, Amos, and Kahneman, Daniel (1981): "The framing of decisions and the psychology of choice," *Science*, 211(4481), 453–458.

Tversky, Amos, and Kahneman, Daniel (1992): "Advances in prospect theory: Cumulative representation of uncertainty," *Journal of Risk and Uncertainty*, 5(4), 297–323.

Tversky, Amos, and Russo, J. Edward (1969): "Substitutability and similarity in binary choices," *Journal of Mathematical Psychology*, 6(1), 1–12.

Volkmann, John (1934): "The relation of the time of judgment to the certainty of judgment," *Psychological Bulletin*, 31(9), 672–673.

Wakker, Peter P. (2010): *Prospect Theory: For Risk and Ambiguity*. Cambridge University Press, Cambridge.

Weber, Elke (2004): "Perception matters: Psychophysics for economists," in *The Psychology of Economic Decisions: Reasons and Choices* (Vol. 2), Brocas, Isabelle, and Carrillo, Juan (Eds.), Oxford University Press, New York, 163–176.

Weber, Ernst (1834): *De Tactu.* (*The Sense of Touch*, translated 1978. Academic Press, New York.)

Weber, Roberto A. (2003): "'Learning' with no feedback in a competitive guessing game," *Games and Economic Behavior*, 44(1), 134–144.

Weil, R. S., Furl, N., Ruff, C. C. et al. (2010): "Rewarding feedback after correct visual discriminations has both general and specific influences on visual cortex," *Journal of Neurophysiology*, 104(3), 1746–1757.

Wichmann, Felix A., and Jäkel, Frank (2018): "Methods in psychophysics," *Stevens' Handbook of Experimental Psychology and Cognitive Neuroscience*, 5(7), 265–306.

Willemsen, Martijn C., and Johnson Eric J. (2019): "(Re) visiting the decision factory: Observing cognition with MouselabWEB," in *A Handbook of Process Tracing Methods*, Schulte-Mecklenbeck, Michael, Kuehberger, Anton, and Johnson, Joseph G. (Eds.), Routledge, New York, 76–95.

Woodford, Michael (2020): "Modeling imprecision in perception, valuation, and choice," *Annual Review of Economics*, 12, 579–601.

Wooldridge, Jeffrey M. (2019): "Correlated random effects models with unbalanced panels," *Journal of Econometrics*, 211(1), 137–150.

Yellott, John I. (1977): "The relationship between Luce's choice axiom, Thurstone's theory of comparative judgment, and the double exponential distribution," *Journal of Mathematical Psychology*, 15(2), 109–144.

Yuksel, Sevgi (2022): "Specialized learning and political polarization," *International Economic Review*, 63(1), 457–474.

Zauberman, Gal, Kim, B. Kyu, Malkoc, Selin A., and Bettman, James R. (2009): "Discounting time and time discounting: Subjective time perception and intertemporal preferences," *Journal of Marketing Research*, 46(4), 543–556.

Zeigenfuse, Matthew D., Pleskac, Timothy J., and Liu, Taosheng (2014): "Rapid decisions from experience," *Cognition*, 131(2), 181–194.

Acknowledgments

We thank Carlos Alós-Ferrer, Roberto Barbera, Rahul Bhui, Jordi Brandts, Mark Dean, Sean Duffy, Roberto Hernán-González, Yamir Moreno, David Pascual-Ezama, María Pereda Garcia, Nuria Rodríguez Priego, Ismael Rodriguez-Lara, and Angel Sánchez for helpful comments. We are particularly grateful to Monica Vasco. Financial support from AEI/MCIN (PID2021-126892NB-I00) and a grant from the Rutgers University–Camden College of Arts and Sciences are gratefully acknowledged.

Cambridge Elements $\equiv$

Behavioural and Experimental Economics

Nicolas Jacquemet
University Paris-1 Panthéon Sorbonne and the Paris School of Economics

Nicolas Jacquemet is a full professor at University Paris-1 Panthéon Sorbonne and the Paris School of Economics. His research combines experimental methods and econometrics to study discrimination, the effect of personality traits on economic behaviour, the role of social pre-involvement in strategic behaviour and experimental game theory. His research has been published in *Econometrica, Management Science, Games and Economic Behavior,* the *Journal of Environmental Economics and Management,* the *Journal of Health Economics,* and the *Journal of Economic Psychology.*

Olivier L'Haridon
Université de Rennes 1

Olivier L'Haridon is a full professor at the Université de Rennes I, France. His research combines experimental methods and decision theory, applied in the study of individual decision making as affected by uncertainty. His work has been published in *American Economic Review, Management Science,* the *Journal of Risk and Uncertainty, Theory and Decision, Experimental Economics,* the *Journal of Health Economics,* and the *Journal of Economic Psychology.*

About the Series

Cambridge Elements in Behavioural and Experimental Economics focuses on recent advances in two of the most important and innovative fields in modern economics. It aims to provide better understanding of economic behavior, choices, strategies and judgements, particularly through the design and use of laboratory experiments.